South Hill Rascals

Once a Rascal

Always A Rascal

JAMES E. GRAHAM

Enjoy!

Jim Graham

James E. Graham
63150 270th Street
Nevada, Iowa 50201

ISBN: 978-1-5356-0303-4

DEDICATION

All but three of our nine grandkids live a thousand miles away. I've been thinking about how to let them know who their grandfather was, how much fun he had growing up, and what a wonderful family we have. The more I thought about it, the more it became clear to me that what I should do is simply tell them the story.

ACKNOWLEDGEMENTS

There is no way that I can ever properly thank Joseph Gill and Mary Harriet (Schiltz) Graham, our father and mother, for all they did to help their four boys to know and become the persons they were intended to be. I hope and know that they are still smiling.

TABLE OF CONTENTS

PREFACE—WHAT IS IN A NAMESAKE?

As I wrote this, I realized that some of the story you will believe, and some of it you may not. I may be able to explain what really happened in a better way, but I am really trying to write the story exactly the way it happened. Everybody who reads *South Hill Rascals* can make up their own minds if this was the wonderful life that I think it was. Before you are finished, you will also understand and know who the Grahams are.

Know how important it is to me that everyone understands what and how it happened. The reader needs to listen to the stories themselves as I tell them to you. In those cases where you have a question or just don't believe what you're reading, ask yourself what really happened. Your guess may or may not be true. Wait until the end of the book before you make up your mind. I would never tell a story that was not completely, absolutely, and totally true––or maybe just once in a while. You decide as you read. Once you have read the book, you will know.

The Random House Dictionary of the English Language defines *namesake* as "a person named after another." My life experience and observation tells me that half of the people in the world are named after someone else. In my case, I was named after the Right Reverend Monsignor Emmett Kelly. In looking through my father's Dubuque,

Iowa, Columbia College memorabilia, it is very clear that my father, Joseph Gill Graham, and Msgr. Kelly were friends for years both before and after Columbia College became Loras College. My middle name, Emmett, came from Father Kelly. My father sang in Msgr. Kelly's all-male college choir. Msgr. Kelly often fished and played cards and horseshoes at Grandpa Edward Graham's Frentress Lake cottage south of East Dubuque, Illinois, as our family memorabilia and pictures show.

In 1956, when I was a senior at Loras Academy, Msgr. Kelly died. A month before Msgr. Kelly died, Dad and I drove to New Hampton, Iowa where Msgr. Kelly was pastor and dean of St. Joseph's Church. Our visit together lasted for an hour before Msgr. Kelly seemed to get tired, so we shook his hand and left. All through the conversation, Msgr. Kelly would occasionally stop and look at me. Then one time he asked me: "James Emmett, I need you to make a promise to me." I told Msgr. Kelly that I would, but he never told me what he wanted me to promise him. The second time he told this to me he stopped for a moment and told me he wanted me to promise that I would do all I could to make the world I was living in a better place. I held his hand in mine and told him I would do my very best. Then he and Dad went back to sharing memories of all the wonderful times they had had together.

When our visit was over and Dad and I were leaving the room, Msgr. Kelly said to me "Jimmy, my boy, I'll see what I can do to help you." Father Kelly knew that when a Graham makes a promise he keeps it. What this Graham didn't know was how Father Kelly would keep his promise to me. When it happened, I knew how he had kept his promise and you will too.

INTRODUCTION
WHY SOUTH HILL RASCALS

I read *Tom Sawyer* when I was in grade school, and I marveled at how much fun Tom Sawyer had when he was just a kid. I never dreamed that I was destined to have a similar meaningful and fun-filled life growing up. As you might suspect, there are many other episodes that bring a smile to my face that were not included in *South Hill Rascals*. The one that keeps coming to my mind was one summer when I was a junior in high school. There was only intermittent or part-time work. My brother Tom; Dick Blasen, my Saint Columbkille grade-school classmate and I decided to build an inboard flat-bottom speedboat with a 1948 V-8 flat-head Ford-powered engine. We built the boat in Dick Blasen's father's garage on Cleveland Avenue.

Think about how difficult that was going to be working from scratch and never having done it before. We knew we had the help of Dick's father who rebuilt the engine for us. No one helped us with the design and construction of the boat or with installing the engine, driveshaft, propeller, steering etc.

Once built, our inboard literally flew across the water. You could not really steer it at that speed, but that didn't really matter. Steering could always be fixed, maybe next year.

It was just a question of learning how to operate the boat. You can usually avoid being sucked into the wake of a Mississippi River barge by hitting the wake at right angles and going straight through and over the other side. It was also helpful not to have screaming girls with you when you were testing what the inboard could do.

After some testing, Tom and I determined that it would probably have been better if we had a reverse gear so we could back up the inboard. Even so, there was nothing about bringing the boat to shore that could not be worked around. All we had to do was jump in the water before the inboard ran up on the shore. It didn't take long before I realized I had to warn Tom *before* we jumped and not *as* we were jumping. If I failed to do that, Tom had a tendency to get really mad. I am sure it would have been worse if Tom didn't make the safety of the water before the inboard ran aground and we had to drag the boat back into the water.

Now that I think about it, we were lucky just to get the finished boat to Frentress Lake on the Illinois side of the Mississippi River. The old trailer we built the inboard on collapsed just as we put the boat into the water. So what? We got it there! We all had the joy of knowing that nothing was impossible. All we needed was the idea and our family and friends to watch and help us once in a while.

It took a long time for me to realize how unbelievably fortunate Tom and I were to have grown up in Dubuque on the Mississippi. Tom Sawyer survived his time on the Mississippi with pluck and luck. My brother Tom and I certainly had our share of both.

South Hill Rascals is my way of thanking everyone and hopefully helping to encourage everyone who reads it to believe in its message.

WITHOUT FURTHER ADO ON WITH THE STORY.

CHAPTER 1—LEARNING THE MEANING OF FAMILY

I went to kindergarten at the Visitation Academy on Alpine Street. My younger brother Tom and I would get up in the morning at Grandpa Harry Schiltz's house on Nevada Street. We were living with Grandpa Harry Schiltz. Dad was serving in the US Navy as a navigator for a minesweeper during World War II. Every morning, Tom and I would wake up and go into the kitchen where Grandpa Harry was already cooking us pancakes with some fruit. Tom and I could not figure out how Grandpa always got up before we did. Grandpa was an old guy and Tom and I knew we were smarter than he was. So we made a plan. We were going to get up before Grandpa and cook him some pancakes with fruit.

The next day we got up half an hour earlier. We couldn't hear anything going on in the house. We ran down the hall to the kitchen and there he was, cooking breakfast. How did that happen? The third day we got up an hour earlier and ran down the hall and there he was. The next day we got up two hours earlier and ran down the hall. There he was. We finally told Grandpa that we loved him, and that *he* was smarter than we were. That was hard for us to say because we thought we were smart too, but we enjoyed breakfast.

After breakfast I had to go to the Visitation Academy for kindergarten. Kindergarten wasn't all that good a deal. Tom could stay home and work with Grandpa while Grandpa was building a house or making cabinets. Grandpa was a very, very good carpenter and he spent a lot of time showing both of us how to use his tools the RIGHT way.

I remember the first day I went to kindergarten. Mom and Mom's father, Grandpa Schlitz, were with me when we met the teacher. My father, Joseph Graham, had two sisters who were nuns at the Visitation Academy. Their names were Sister Mary Irene and Sister Mary Patricia, but neither one was my kindergarten teacher. That day we walked from Grandpa's house across the street and across the Nativity churchyard next door about a block away to the school. The first thing I noticed when we got into the classroom was that there were these alien creatures called GIRLS. My mom had all boys: me, Tom, and our two little brothers, Joe and John. No girls. I didn't know what this was going to be like with girls. The teacher seemed to be nice and I thought that I would give it a try and see how everything went.

Mom always told me that I had to be nice to girls. Dad told me that if I ever hit a girl he would give me a penalty so large it would go into the record books.

The girls were different. They kept asking the teacher if there was something that they could do to help her. They kept asking the teacher if what they were doing was just exactly the way she wanted them to do it. One girl, Judy Gavin was her name, even asked the teacher if there was some way she could help the teacher. I had never been in a situation like this before where I had to listen to all of that nonsense. Even so, the teacher seemed to help me whenever I needed it. I began to think that maybe everything would work out all right.

The best part of the morning was when we had recess where the whole class went out behind the school. We could play basketball if we wanted. Or we could just talk like the girls all seemed to do. One day, I noticed this huge smokestack that went up taller than the three-story school building. It was really high! I got to thinking, *What would the world look like if I could see it from way up there?* The problem was how I could get high enough to reach the ladder. The ladder that was on the side of the smokestack didn't have any rungs until it got 10 feet above the ground. There were no ladders or anything that you could use to reach up that high. I got to thinking. There was one girl in the class who was almost a foot taller than the rest of the girls. It was Judy Gavin.

The next day I said hi to Judy and asked her how she liked kindergarten. She said she really enjoyed it and she was learning a lot. I told her that I enjoyed it also, and it was nice to have her in our class. For a couple of days, I asked Judy some questions and we talked about a whole lot of things.

Then, one day when we were all out behind the school, I stopped in front of the smokestack. I looked up and got a sad expression on my face. I didn't say anything. I just stood there looking up. Judy came up to me and asked me what was wrong. I told her that I really wanted to see what the world looked like from way up there, but I didn't know how to get up there. The first rung was just too high for me to jump and catch it. Judy said to me: "Maybe I can help you. Why don't you stand on my shoulders and maybe then you can reach the rung."

Judy did just what I had asked her to do. I put one foot on her hip, the next foot on her shoulder and I could reach it! It was easy to climb the ladder, rung after rung higher and higher and higher.

Finally I got to the top. What a gorgeous sight! I could see the church across the street. I could even see Grandpa Schiltz's house on the other side of the church! I was taller than the trees and the bushes looked like little things down on the ground. I was really glad I was up there.

Looking down I could see Judy. She was waving at me. I could also see that there were three nuns in the playground and they were running around in circles. They would stop and talk to one another for a second, move in different directions and then come back and talk again. Once in a while, one of the nuns would point up. I may not have been the smartest kid in the world, but something told me I was in trouble. The more I thought about it, the more I realized it was not in my best interest to go back down the ladder. I looked all around. It was a beautiful day. I wasn't really hungry. I could see the birds coming in and out of the trees. The flat part of the top of the smokestack was pretty wide. Maybe I could just lie down and take a nap?

Then I saw one of the nuns lead the crowd taking all of the kids back in the school. I knew that something was up. Later I found out they called Grandpa Schultz and asked him to come over in his pickup and he did. Grandpa looked up and yelled, "Hey Jim, you want to get some lunch?" I said yes and came down. The subject never came up again. The next day we went out to play. I noticed that someone had taken off two more steel rungs on the smokestack. You could tell because there were shiny spots where the rungs had been sawed off.

There was one other thing I didn't really understand when I was in kindergarten. On weekends Mom and Dad would take Tom and me to the Visitation High School Academy to visit with Sister Irene and Sister Patricia. Sister Irene taught both the violin and the viola. Sister Patricia taught the piano and singing. Almost every time when we made the visit Grandma and Grandpa Graham were there too. Grandpa Ed Graham and his wife, Irene, were Irish and I would sing Irish songs for them. Grandpa Graham's favorite song was "Danny Boy." The other song he liked a lot was "Galway Bay."

I never understood why as I sang "Danny Boy" Grandpa Graham would cry. I didn't think that I was that bad a singer. Sister Patricia said I had a beautiful voice. After I finished "Danny Boy," Grandpa would give me a hug. It NEVER made any sense to me why someone would cry over a song. After I grew up a little, I realized that Grandpa was Irish and he had probably sung that song when he was a boy. I really liked to sing! Those were nice weekends when we visited Sister Irene and Sister Patricia.

MARBLES AT NATIVITY CHURCH GRADE SCHOOL ON ALPINE STREET

I went to the Nativity Church Grade School for first grade right across the street from Grandpa Harry's house at 125 Nevada Street. Across the street from Grandpa's house was a grassy area next to the building where many kids played marbles. There must've been ten, twelve, or fifteen kids playing marbles at the same time. Everyone had a sack full of marbles. Some of them were beautiful sacks, multicolored with a fancy pull-string on the top. One of the kids had a double-sized sack. He won marbles from everyone. He invited anybody who was dumb enough to play with him so that he could add to his marble bag. This looked like an opportunity for me to have some real fun playing with someone who thought he was God's favorite child. I asked Grandma Mary Schiltz if she would get me some marbles, and she said she would. If Grandma Schiltz says she'll do something you can count on it.

The very next day I got a sack of nondescript marbles with not one, but two shooters.

I asked my brother Tom if he would be my victim in my effort to learn how to play marbles. Tom informed me that the only victim was going to be me. He fully intended to win all the marbles from me. We played for hours the first day. It was a draw. The second day we started early. I learned a new way to shoot that was straighter and had a little more power. Tom figured out his own way to shoot and we were tied. No one was the winner. Then I settled down and concentrated on making every shot count and something began to happen. Tom and I played for another week. I finally knew I was ready.

The next day at recess I came up to the guy who had the big, beautiful sack of marbles and asked him if he would be kind enough to let me donate marbles to him with the understanding that first he had to win them. My first thought was that I would let him shoot first and that would break up all the marbles so that each one could then be the subject of a special individual shot. He broke them up and got eight or nine marbles out of the circle. But then he missed. I took my special shooter and got my first marble out. Then I got another one and shot again. I got another one and another one and another one. Finally there was only one marble left. I stood up, stretched, yawned, knelt down and killed it.

The guy never knew what hit him. I assured him it must've been beginner's luck. I didn't use the word anomaly because I didn't know what the word was. One way or another I talked him into doing it again. Wonder of wonders, this time I got to shoot first and I got a marble out the first shot. Then I cleaned up with about three left before I missed. The bell rang and we had to go back to class. I told him that I was looking forward to playing with him again tomorrow.

In about a week, maybe it was a week and a half, I had everybody's marbles and I had the biggest sack you can imagine.

But then I had a problem. I was invited, or directed, to come to the office of the principal. She was a nice person, Sister Mary something. I don't remember what her name really was. Anyway, Sister said to me, "Well, Jim, I know you are a good marble player but I also know that you are a good person. I have had your classmates come into my office. They were crying because they no longer had any marbles. I asked them if you won them fairly or whether you were cheating and they said you won them fairly. That was not the point. She told me: "THESE are your classmates. You should be doing things that make them love you so they can continue to have a good time with you." Then she asked me the awful question. "Jim, what are you going to do with your marbles?" I looked at her and I thought about it before saying: "I think I'm going to give their marbles back to them. Sister got up off of her chair, came around her desk and gave me a hug.

When I think about it, the time I spent with Grandma and Grandpa Schiltz when Dad was in the navy was a wonderful time. After school, and especially on weekends, Tom and I would ride in the back of Grandpa Schlitz's construction company pickup truck. Grandpa would ride all around the city and talk to his people who were building houses. They were doing work for Grandpa and his son Jack, who also worked for him. Tom and I had to sit down in the back of the truck and put ropes around us so that if he had to stop quickly, we would still be okay. Grandpa didn't know that we never tied the ropes. When he stopped, we were out of the truck immediately and looking over what was to be seen. Everybody knew us when we came, and they all loved Grandpa. Before the day was over, Grandma would always stop in a place where we could eat. Tom and I both enjoyed ice cream. We never told Mom because she didn't want us to eat too many sweets. Thinking back on it, I now know Mom knew exactly what we were doing. She must have smiled about it!

Mom knew exactly what we were doing all the time! I wasn't really aware of this for quite a while. Then one day Mom came into our bedroom and stood next to our bunkbed—I slept on the top bunk and Tom on the bottom. She said, "Thank you boys for helping the Rudzianskis today." Bobby Rudzianski was our buddy. His family lived two doors north on the same side of 135 South Hill Street where we lived. It only took us an hour to clean up and clean out Mr. Rudzianski's garage. This was no big deal. Besides, we had cookies and ice cream just for being helpful. There was no way that Mom could ever have known about that, but she did. Tom and I did a lot of things for cookies and ice cream.

RHODE ISLAND WITH MOM AND DAD

Tom and the Crawdad Creek

When we lived in Rhode Island, I was seven in 1944 or 1945 and Tom was six. We lived in an apartment house while Dad was stationed at the naval base nearby. There were a few kids in the neighborhood to play with but not many. Sometimes Dad would have the weekend off when he was not out to sea. We would do some sightseeing along the coast of the Atlantic Ocean. Some of the boys in the neighborhood were about our size and there were a few girls in the neighborhood as well. Mom showed Tom and me how to walk the mile from our house to the school. Once we got close to the school, there was a big creek with a walking bridge over it. You could see fish swimming in the creek. Once in a while there was a tadpole moving around. The birds flitted in and out of the bushes nearby. It was a pretty scene.

The creek was a problem for Tom. He always wanted to stop and see if he could catch fish with his hands. He also captured crawdads and tadpoles and put them in his pocket. When Tom got to school, he would put the crawdads and tadpoles in the desk of one of the girls in the classroom. She would scream and the teacher was not happy. But nobody knew exactly who did it. I told Tom that he better stop doing that because sooner or later they would find out it was him and he would be in trouble. He didn't care and there was nothing I could do about it.

I remember one day after Tom had so much fun with the crawdads I started to have trouble talking him into going to school. He would stay at the creek and play with whatever would move. I told Tom to come with me because we are going to be late for school. He didn't do it. I went to school anyway and the teacher asked me where Tom was. I told her that he was at the creek so she sent one of his classmates to go get him. When the classmate told Tom to come to school, he informed the classmate that he was not ready yet. The classmate made a fatal mistake by trying to force Tom to go, and Tom gave him a black eye. The teacher was concerned, but I told her that I would go get Tom, and I did. Tom didn't like it but he knew better than to play with me.

The Local Gang Problem

It seemed like Tom and I were together all day every day. A mile to school didn't seem very long, but it took a while if you are taking your time and looking at neighborhood dogs or whatever else there was to look at. There really wasn't any reason to run home. In our trips we noticed there were a lot of kids hanging around a street corner. They didn't say hi to us and we didn't say hi to them. We just walked on by. I got to thinking about what we would do if those four or five guys started to cause us trouble. Dad once told us that if you have to deal with more than one guy, you have to stay moving so that several people don't have a clear shot at you at the same time.

Tom and I decided that we would wolf, or slowly circle back to back and try to knock people off balance so that he or I could give them a really good smack. We never thought much about it until one day four guys stood between us and the way to our house. There was much conversation from the guy who appeared to be the leader. He explained to us that this was their neighborhood and that we needed to either join his club or there would be consequences.

I told the leader that Tom and I were too ugly to join their group and that they were better off just to leave us alone. As they moved toward us, Tom and I smacked the first two and then moved back to back and slowly circled. I would knock someone off balance and Tom would smack him right in the eye. At the same time Tom would do the same thing for me. After two of their gang got hit, we straightened out and went directly for the other two and they ran. After that we didn't have any trouble with any of the neighbor kids.

Then one day as I was walking home I ran into the leader of the gang. He walked up to me, never said a word and punched me in the jaw. It knocked me off balance. He must have hit me five times before I could fully regain my balance. I moved off to his left and got away from him. When I got home Mom didn't say a thing. There I was all bruised and bloodied up. I sat down at the kitchen table and Mom took a wet rag and cleaned me up. She didn't say a thing until finally she asked, "Do you think you can take him?" I thought for a second and told her: "Yes." Mom explained that at this point it was just between him and me, and I needed to try to keep it that way by settling it between the two of us. It would be unfair for me to bring Tom so that we would be two against one. All he would do is bring more of his gang to try to teach the two of us who was the neighborhood boss.

I asked Mom how she knew this. She told me she had four brothers and listened to them solving similar problems. Years later I learned that Uncle Howie was an engineer and he became a three-star general in the US Army. Her other brother, LaVern, was also an engineer in the US Army and he was the City Engineer for Dubuque.

Mom and I walked down the street to the kid's house together. I knocked on his front door. His mother was there and I asked if he would come out and talk to me. As he got to the edge of his porch and took the first step down I hit him as hard as I could right in the jaw right in front of his mother. Then I hit him five or ten times before his mother showed up with a big broom and I left. I don't know where my mother was. She was gone. I never had any trouble with the gang leader again.

The Minesweeper Kite

One day after Tom and I woke up, had breakfast and went outside, we noticed the neighbor had a huge kite way up above his house. The kite had a tail that looked like it was made out of rags or maybe some rope. They seemed to know what they were doing and were able to make the kite jerk up and down and wave from left to right in the sky. They laughed and gave one another chances to try to make the kite fly. This went on for maybe an hour until they finally got tired of it. Tom said to me, "You know, that seemed to be a pretty small kite." It didn't get much higher in the sky than their house was. We wondered what it would be like if we had a big kite and it flew way above the house where the wind was really tall. The more we thought about that, the more we really wanted to do it.

When Dad came home that night from the minesweeper that he was a navigator on, we asked him if he had ever built a kite and told him what we wanted to do. Dad looked at us a little bit funny, didn't say anything for a while. Then he had an idea. We could tell because he had an evil grin on his face and he looked at us funny. He said, "Boys, the neighbors don't even know what a kite is. On the minesweeper we have a big balloon that flies three hundred feet high in the sky to protect the minesweeper from airplanes. Our house is forty-five feet high and the balloon flies three hundred feet high. Do you have any idea how high that is?" I looked at Tom, he looked at me, and we both said, "No." Dad told us: "Tomorrow is Friday. My ship won't be leaving the harbor. Let's go to the ship and I'll show you what I'm talking about."

The next day we went to the navy base. Sure enough, there was Dad's minesweeper. He talked to the guard and the guard let us on the ship. Dad showed us the blimp, how it was blown up, and he blew it up on the shortest line he could. Then he pointed out that there was some used line they no longer needed. He thought it would be a good idea if we took that line and used it for the kite. That's what we thought we would do, and we did it.

The next day was Saturday. Tom, Dad and I got up and went out to the garage where there was a small pile of wooden house siding. The siding was about six inches wide by maybe three-quarters of an inch thick and ten feet long. Dad took the siding down into the basement and cut the wooden framework for a kite that was as big as he was. We are talking about a six-foot kite from side to side and maybe an eight-foot kite from bottom to top. Dad used his wood plane to make sure that both the cross-section length and width were what they should be. Instead of nailing the wood together he tied them together with some really strong rope. We all went downtown to a store that sold all kinds of tools and household things and bought some really long rolls of thick, strong paper.

When Dad finally put the kite together it was a foot taller than he was, not counting the six-foot-long tail. He bent and bowed the kite arms both left and right so that it could fly. The bow's cross-arm line was really strong. Sunday was going to be the magic trial. We all had a Saturday supper, talked about things and tried to sleep. Tom and I weren't able to sleep because we were thinking about how much fun it was going to be.

Sunday we got up and went to church. When we got back we reminded Dad that he had promised us to help us fly the kite. He admitted that he had done so, and we went out to this little park that was about a half a block away. There weren't many trees and everything was just an open park and a playground. Dad had this huge long line. It must've been six or seven hundred feet of line. We wound the end of the line around a couple of wooden pegs, anchoring the kite line to a teeter-totter in the park. I held one side of the kite and Tom held the other side. Sure enough it took off and went up and up and up. It was amazing! We didn't have the common sense to have a camera with us. It was just fun flying the kite. We got it almost to the end of the line. Soon there was a huge burst of wind WAY UP there and the line broke about halfway up to the kite.

I never hesitated. I ran toward the street trying to follow the kite. It was flipping back and forth and flying away and away and away. I ran down the street. The kite was going fast. I looked back and saw that there was a kid on a motorcycle coming toward me. I stepped out in front of him so he had to stop. I pointed to the kite and told him what happened and asked him if he would take me to where the kite came down. He looked at me funny but said yes. So I got on the back of the motorcycle. We zipped through the town until we saw where the kite had stopped. It was on top of a two-story flat-roofed school building. I thanked him for the ride, looked at the building and thought: *How am I going to get on top of that building?*

On the side of the building there were three big vines that went from the ground all the way to the top. One of those vines looked like it was pretty strong. I started climbing, trying to choose the strongest of the vines as I climbed up. I got to the top of the building and saw that the kite was not damaged. I was able to lower the kite down the side of the building to the ground. By the time I got down off the roof, I lifted the kite off the ground and took it to the road. Dad was there with our car and we took the kite home. Tom and I never forgot how neat and wonderful that whole experience was. We both thought that when the war was finally over and we went back to Dubuque, we would have Dubuque's best kite. We would fly it over the Mississippi River from the cliffs far up on Eagle Point Park. When we arrived in Dubuque after the war was over, Tom and I looked for the kite and found out that Mom and Dad did not bring it with them. We had other things to do but I will never forget the kite.

GRANDPA GRAHAM'S FARM ON CEDAR CROSS ROAD

Food Heaven

There was a time in Dubuque when I think I was ten and my brother Tom was nine. At least I think that's how old we were. It doesn't really matter when you're living it. Mom and Dad decided it would be a good idea for Tom, me, and our two little brothers, Joe and John, to spend the summer at Grandpa Graham's farm. That was the year when there was a polio epidemic even in Dubuque. The farm was a really, really good idea. The farmhouse was on the east side of Cedar Cross Road—a gravel road that ran north and south separating the farmhouse on the east from the barn on the west side of the road. The farmhouse roadside had a beautiful white fence with a big, flowered entrance gate to the house. The barn was a story and a half high, had stables for the horses on the south side and room for the three cows on the north side. In between was a big open space from floor to roof for all the feed and the hay mow.

Grandpa Graham's farm was a wonderful place. At the back of the house there were apple trees, peach trees and cherry trees. My favorite plants were on the east of the house. We called them tomatoes. Both Tom and I carried a salt shaker in our pockets everywhere we went. If we could not reach the peaches or the apples or the cherries, we used the horses. I am not saying that we ate all day long but there might be some small element of truth in that. By far our favorites were the tomatoes. We learned that if we bent forward while we were eating the tomatoes they wouldn't drip down on our shirts. It was an opportunity to avoid explaining to Mom how we got them so dirty.

It did not take Tom or me long to figure out that it was in our best interest to keep tomato juice off of our shirts and pants. What Mom would do is take us onto the porch where she had filled a big tub with ice-cold well water. We would be naked as a jaybird sitting in a frozen tub. It was a good week when Tom and I could avoid a bath.

Tomatoes were not the only problem. Grandma's brother, Uncle Charlie, grew a field of strawberries. I remember them saying that the field was an acre. Tom and I were required to pick and box strawberries for Uncle Charlie. Uncle Charlie had a huge pile of small wooden boxes for the strawberries. He counted what we did every day. Uncle Charlie was a good man. We did not want him to get into trouble so Tom and I always picked the thirty boxes that he needed every day. What we didn't tell Uncle Charlie was that we ate a couple boxes every day. Thinking back on it, I cannot believe that Uncle Charlie didn't know what we were doing.

Brownie, Our Sheepdog

One of the nicest animals and best friends that my brother Tom and I ever had while we were on the farm was Brownie, our sheep dog. Every day when we woke up, Brownie met us at the side door. Brownie would jump up and put his front legs on my shoulders and give me a morning kiss. Then he would go to my brother Tom and try to do the same thing. Tom would wrestle with him until they were both on the ground. Wherever we were, Brownie was. When we rode the horses, Brownie was always running along next to us. Sometimes when we stopped, Brownie would circle the horses at full speed just for the fun of it until we told him to stop. Whenever we stopped riding the horses to give them a rest, Brownie was never more than two feet away from either Tom or me. Brownie was truly our brother in fun.

When we played in the barn climbing the hay, Brownie was ahead of us. When we were picking berries in the field for Uncle Charlie, Brownie always tried one berry but just spit it out. Brownie looked at us funny when we ate the berries but one berry was enough for him. In the evening after dinner, Grandma, Grandpa, Mom and Dad would sit on the porch on the south side of the house. Brownie was always with Tom and me lying nearby while Grandma and Grandpa told us stories or talked about what happened that day. I once asked Grandpa if dogs went to heaven. Grandpa looked at Brownie. Then he looked at me and told me that friends are always together in heaven. That was good enough for me.

Francis the Jack-Eyed Mule

One of the funniest animals that Grandpa had was a little mule that he called Francis. I don't remember where Francis came from. If we were on the same side of the farm as Francis, we would always put some bailing twine over his head and one of us would ride him.

Francis liked it. I remember in the spring when the field on the house side of the farm road was still pretty bumpy. We wanted to tie our wagon to Francis and run around the field like in a chariot. Tom and I thought it would be a smart thing for us to test it first to see if it would work. We decided to put our younger brothers, Joe and John, in the wagon and see what happened. We figured out how to make the chariot connection from Francis to the wagon. We put Joe and John in the wagon and gave Joe the two reins. We yelled and Francis started running. The wagon bounced up and down the whole way. Finally, Joe and John fell out of the wagon and Francis dragged the wagon upside down across the rest of the field.

Our Horses, Birdie and Rebel

Grandpa had four horses. Two of the horses were Morgans. They were both reddish-brown wonderful riding horses. Tom and I never got to ride either Quinn or Dusty. Only Grandpa Ed Graham and our dad, Joe Graham, got to ride the two Morgans. The other two horses were available to Tom and me. The prettiest horse was named Birdie. She was a western quarter horse. Birdie was the mother of the last horse, named Jack. Jack was a big horse. His father must have been a big work horse. Jack also had a problem with his left eye so Grandpa would not let us ride him. That left only one horse for two of us, and that was Birdie. We had a wonderful western saddle and all day to ride and we did. Tom was smaller and younger than I so he did not get as much time on Birdie as I did. You can imagine the whining from Tom that Grandma and Grandpa and Mom and Dad had to put up with at the dinner table. It was a daily topic of conversation.

Tom and I did not know it but Grandpa was looking for a horse for Tom. The problem was that Tom's horse had to be the most docile and laid-back animal in Dubuque County. Tom was not laid-back and docile and they were afraid he would get hurt. One day a pickup truck pulled up towing a horse trailer. This was just after dinner. Mom and Dad and Grandpa and Grandma and Tom and I and little brothers Joe and John all went out to meet the driver. I looked into the horse trailer and saw that there was a big painted pony asleep in the trailer. I could tell because the pony's nose was touching the floor and he was not moving. The man who brought the horse dropped the back gate and led the pony down the gate where the pony's nose touched the ramp as it was coming down out of the trailer.

Dad shook Grandpa's hand. They both shook the hand of the man who brought the painted pony. Everybody went back into the house except Tom and I. We took the pony behind the barn where there were two great big circular wire grain bins. You could see the corn in the pen still on their husks. Tom stopped the horse and asked me: "What should we name the horse?" I told Tom that it was his horse and that he should name it. He thought for a minute and then he said: "I know what it should be. We will call him Rebel."

At this point, Rebel was standing with his nose next to the ground half asleep. Tom went behind the grain bin and picked up about a three foot stick and stood in front of the semi sleeping Rebel. He looked straight at the horse and screamed: "WAKE UP!" at the same time hitting the horse on the forehead with the stick. The horse dropped to his front knees, stayed there for a minute. He finally opened his eyes and looked straight at Tom staring at him. Rebel leaped to his feet. Tom did not put a saddle on him. He just jumped on Rebel and they ran away down the lane to the pasture.

The next day when Grandpa Graham came back from work, he looked down the lane to the pasture and he saw me on Birdie and Tom on Rebel. We were both racing up to the house for dinner. He could not believe his eyes. The paint was racing ahead of Birdie. He shook his head and went into the house.

Birdie and Rebel and Tom and I became good friends. The horses would wait every morning next to the barn pasture fence where they could see Tom and me coming out of the farmhouse after breakfast. We would get a bucket, feed them some grain every morning, and made sure they had access to the water trough. We would brush them down every day and once in a while we would steal an apple for them.

Tom and I often worked in the fields, next to the pasture, picking strawberries for Uncle Charlie or cutting weeds in the hay field or helping Uncle Charlie bale hay. The horses always grazed in the pasture near the fence where we could see one another. Tom and I knew that Birdie and Rebel liked us and believed in us. We were not *just* good friends. We loved and trusted one another.

CATFISH CREEK

Tom, Rebel, and the Fence

Every morning Tom and I would get up, gobble our pancakes and fruit, stuff a salt shaker in a pocket and go saddle the horses. Every morning both Birdie and Rebel waited at the fence across the road near the gate to their pasture. They waited for us to give them their morning apple. If it was raining, we would put the horses in the barn where we would feed and water them and play in the barn's hay loft.

We had a western saddle for Rebel. This made it possible for Tom to hang on to the saddle while racing the horses or turning the horses sharply around trees or whatever else he wanted to do. We really didn't need a saddle but it helped. All we really had to do was hold onto the horses' manes and use our heels to keep us stable. One morning we set off down the pasture to the far west end of the farm right next to

25

Catfish Creek where the farm fence was. We had raced around our side of the fence many times chasing Brownie or one another.

On this day, we had a different idea. We heard Mom, Dad, Grandpa and Grandma talking about how beautiful the Catfish Creek area is but we had never seen it. Tom and I decided we were going to figure out how to get over that fence. We got down off the horses and looked at the top barbed wire. Incredibly, we found that it was loose along three fence posts. If we pulled the top wire down, the fence was only two feet high. We both agreed that these horses were perfectly capable of jumping that low fence.

I got on Birdie and ran back east toward the farmhouse. Birdie stretched out and she was flying. Once she got to full speed, I turned her around and headed straight for the fence. Just before the fence I kicked her in the side and she jumped it. I looked at Tom. Tom got on Rebel and did the same thing. When Rebel got within one step of the fence, he buried his feet in the ground right at the fence, put his head down and slammed to a stop. Tom flew over the fence, somersaulted and landed on his feet. Rebel looked at Tom and Tom looked at Rebel. Tom jumped the fence and grabbed Rebel's bridle. Tom screamed at Rebel and the horse fully understood that Tom was mad.

After a second or two Tom got back on Rebel, kicked him in the side and headed toward the farmhouse away from the fence. When Rebel got to full speed Tom turned him hard around and headed straight for the fence again. At the last second Tom kicked Rebel in the side. This time Rebel jumped the fence. We were not about to waste this opportunity to explore Catfish Creek, so we headed straight for it.

Swimming at Catfish Creek with the Horses

The first time we took the horses to Catfish Creek for a whole day we just kind of rode around to look things over. The creek was a beautiful place. There was lush grass on both sides of the creek. There was nothing straight about the creek either. In some places, instead of going straight south to the Mississippi River it wandered east and then west across the entire valley. One of the most interesting parts was almost straight down from Grandpa's farm. The east part of the creek bank stood six or seven feet higher than the water in the creek. The west part of the creek bank was almost level or just a little bit higher than the water level itself. I think that Tom and I spent the afternoon exploring up and down the high bank side of the creek and found what appeared to be a good swimming hole. We got a long tree branch and stuck it in the water. The water was deeper than the branch was long and the branch went six feet into the water.

It was really hot that day and we thought it would be a good idea to go swimming. The more we thought about it, we couldn't think of any reason why the horses should not swim with us. So Tom and I took the saddles off of Birdie and Rebel and tried to ride them into the water on the low bank side into the water. They would not go into the water. So we backed up away from the creek, got them running toward the creek but they still stopped before they got into the water. We looked at each other and got an idea.

We put the saddles back on the horses and crossed the creek where the creek banks were low. We rode back east, toward the farm, until we got on the high side of this wonderful swimming hole. We backed the horses away from the swimming hole until we were almost to the trees at the edge of the flat part of the creek bottom. I kicked Birdie with my bare feet. Tom did the same to Rebel. Both horses ran straight for the creek's cliff. As they got to within five feet of the edge, both horses stopped. We almost fell off the horses and could not get them to go any closer to the cliff.

Brownie never hesitated. He leaped off the high bank and splashed into the water. He swam to the low side of the swimming hole, walked onto dry ground, turned around to face us, and shook the water from his hair. He just stood there ready to do it again.

I looked at Tom and he looked at me. We decided we would try something different. We rode back down the high bank side of the creek a long way. We stopped the horses and turned them around to face up the creek to the swimming hole. We got those horses running flat out! When we got up the creek to where the water hole was we jerked the reins to the left and kicked them again. Two steps later they were in the air and in the water.

The splash was higher than the high creek bank itself. The horses went straight to the bottom of the water and pushed themselves straight up. Tom and I both fell off the horses. I was laughing so hard I had a hard time catching Birdie's reins, but I did. We looked around and there were snakes and crawdads swimming on the surface of the pond. The horses walked out of the water and stood there shaking themselves. We looked at each other and yelled: "Yeah!" That was a good day!

First Humans to Climb Catfish Creek Rock Butte

After Tom and I figured out how to get over the bottom pasture fence, we spent a lot of time at Catfish Creek. Rebel and Birdie always liked to get a drink. So the first stop we made was at the creek. After the horses had a drink, we started exploring the creek always heading north where both creek sides were flat with grass. We would stop once in a while to let the horses eat some. One day we were about a half a mile north when we came upon a huge rock butte. It stood in front of us like a skyscraper.

If I remember right, it must have been two or maybe three stories high. It was at least as tall as Grandma and Grandpa Graham's farmhouse. If you stood in front of the butte, you could see it was a very big circle. We rode the horses around it and found the whole thing to be half as big as a football field was wide. On both the south and the north sides of the butte, vines started at the ground and went all the way up to the top. These first vines were really small and there was no way that Tom or I could climb up them to the top. But there were two vines that started ten or twelve feet up from the bottom of the butte. They looked strong enough for us to climb them.

We tied Rebel and Birdie to the small vines and stood on the saddles to reach the big vines. We climbed the vines carefully by pulling down on the vine above us before we put our whole weight on it. We took our time climbing. Pretty soon we actually got to the top. It was a big place full of bushes and small trees. We started to explore it by walking around the outer edges and then a little farther inside. It was clear to both Tom and I that no human being had ever been on this high butte! There was some grass but no berries or anything that was edible.

When we got to the middle of the huge butte, there was a small open space. In the open space there were a dozen rocks in a circle and the circle was full of blacked branches. It had been a long time since anyone had been where we were, but it was now clear that we were *not* the first ones up there! After we had seen enough, we climbed down the strong branches, got on the horses, and continued to explore Catfish Creek until finally it was so late we had to go back to the farm for dinner.

When we got to the farmhouse, everybody was in the kitchen. Grandma Graham and Mom really knew how to cook. We could smell it even outside before we got into the house. Dad and Grandpa Graham talked about having a hard time getting their message across while talking with several people throughout the day. They both shared the details of the conversation and finally

Grandpa said to Dad: "You know, Joe, you can lead a horse to water but you can't force it to drink."

Tom looked at me and I looked at Tom. We both had a puzzled expression on our faces. Tom didn't say anything. He just nodded to me. The food was good but as soon as we were finished we left the kitchen, crossed the road and entered the fence gate in the barn's pasture where the horses were. Tom put a rope around Rebel's head and walked him over to the big water trough. It was a big circular trough. If Tom stood in it, it would come up to his belt. All the horses could drink from it at the same time. So could the cows for that matter. Tom took Rebel to the trough and put Rebel's head over it so he could drink.

Rebel just stood there. Tom put his arms around Rebel's head and leaned his full weight on Rebel's head to try to make him drink. The harder Tom pulled down, the harder Rebel tried to keep his head straight. Tom asked me for help. I grabbed hold of Rebel's head from the other side and put my full weight on his head. It didn't do any good. Rebel just stood there and refused to drink. While I was still trying to get Rebel to drink, Tom left the water trough and went over to the grain bins and picked up a stick. When Tom got back to the water trough, he whacked Rebel on the head with the stick. Rebel fell on his front knees with his head in the water. But he didn't drink. As Rebel stood up, we both gave up and walked away. Tom said to me, "You know, Jim, Grandpa Graham was right. You can't force a horse to drink." The more we talked about it, we came to realize that if Grandpa knew we were mean to Rebel he would take the horses away from us. That really wasn't the point. We both decided that you can't do that to a friend.

THINNING THE CATS

O ne Christmas Tom and I got brand-new BB guns for target practice. They were lever-action cowboy guns. We got really good at shooting. There were not many targets on the farm but we could always find something to shoot at. One day we were both on the road next to the barn when Grandpa Graham saw a cat jump out of the second-floor barn door onto the hood of his car. He and Dad were talking together and we heard him say that we just had too many cats around here.

Tom and I looked at one another. We decided that we were responsible to help Grandpa get rid of some of those cats. We went into the barn and noticed that in the middle of the barn hay was strewn all over. If we piled all of the hay into the west end of the barn, it would be ten or twelve feet high. It was at least high enough so that a cat could jump from the top of the stacked hay in the back of the barn onto the long, high rail that ran from the back of the barn east to the road. This is where the hay wagon would be parked when Uncle Charlie filled in the barn with hay. A cat could run along the rail to the east end of the barn where we could get a good shot at it with our BB guns.

We figured that if you shot a cat running on the rail east to the road in the butt with a BB gun, it would sting long enough to motivate the cat to continue to run. The plan was the cat would jump out of the open high hay door, land in the road and keep running. Then we'd have one less cat in the barn.

We figured if we could get all the cats together at the at the west end of the barn in the hay pile we could scare the cats out of the stacked hay onto the rail one at a time. Hopefully they would run from the west end of the barn across the rail east to the open roadside door to get away. We spent all morning stacking the hay and chasing cats into the stacked hay. Shortly before Grandpa got home from work, Tom took a pitchfork to the stacked hay. Sure enough the first cat jumped up to the rail and started running east to the road on the rail. I was ready, took careful aim and fired the BB gun. I hit the cat in the butt just as the cat jumped out the door. As luck would have it, Grandpa was just stepping out of his car when the cat landed on the top of his car and then just kept running down the road as we had planned.

Grandpa ran into the barn and saw what we were doing just as Dad pulled up in his car. Tom and I tried to explain to them what we were doing and why we were doing it. It didn't do any good. Dad explained that cats were needed on the farm to kill mice that hid in the barn where Grandma and Uncle Charlie milked the cows. Dad told us that BB guns were for target practice and hunting things to eat and that BB guns were not to be used to hurt or kill animals. Dad took both of our BB guns and told us that we were not going to get them back until we became older and wiser. Whatever that meant?

Things kind of went on as normal on the farm for quite a while. We were looking for games to play and things to do with the horses and decided we would become horse warriors. Now, everybody knows that you can't be a horse warrior unless you have a weapon to fight with. So we went into the woods and cut some limbs to make bows and plenty of arrows. It took us a long time to make the bows. Uncle Charlie had to help us shape the wood so that it would work as a bow. It wasn't all that hard to make the arrows. There were plenty of straight sticks. All you had to do was to shave the stick down leaving a thick head on the end. We had plenty of chicken feathers we could use. After about a week we both had everything we needed to be horse warriors.

It took us quite a while to really be good shots with our new weapons. After a week or two, we could pretty much hit whatever we were aiming at as long as it was no more than twenty feet away. Then we took our skills to the next level. We got on the horses and ran them past whatever we were using as targets trying to hit them on the run. That took a couple weeks longer but we were finally able to do it. The neatest part of the whole thing was that we learned how to steer the horses with our feet and knees. We did not have to use the reins.

Then one day we decided we would play a war game. The perfect place to play the war game was in the orchard next to the south side of the yard. There were four rows of apple trees and some mulberry trees. There must have been fifteen or twenty feet between trees. It was easy to guide the horses from tree row to tree row. With a little practice we got the horses to run around the trees and from row to row at almost a run.

We needed to find out who was the best horse warrior. Tom and I both had at least a dozen arrows in a little pouch we had on our backs. If there ever was a place where we had to guide the horses with our feet and knees, this was it. It was not as easy as we thought it would be. It was hard to keep our balance. The horses moved in one direction as we tried to aim the bow to hit one another. I was almost halfway through my arrows before I began to even come close to hitting Tom. He had the same problem. After we had been doing this for a half an hour or so, I was down to my last arrow. I kicked Birdie, took careful aim and then got knocked completely off my horse by a tree limb I didn't duck. There I was lying on the ground unconscious with Birdie standing over me eating the orchard grass.

Tom later told me that he came over and tried to wake me up but I didn't move. Finally, Tom realized he had to go back to the farmhouse and get help. Tom was not dumb. He knew he had to hide the bows and arrows before he went to the farmhouse. Mom, Grandma and Grandpa came running into the orchard. They stood me up and got me walking slowly to the farmhouse. I don't remember much after that, except that Dad found the bows and arrows and we were forbidden to shoot one another ever again.

Dad explained to us that people were God's children and that Tom and I had to protect one another. While we may not have intended to hurt one another, it could have happened. He told us that only stupid, mean or bad people shot at their brothers or other people where they could really hurt them.

Tom and I were really sad when summer was over and we had to go back to school. Thinking about this time always brings a smile to my face, and I find myself saying thank you to Mom and Dad and Grandpa and Grandma Graham.

LIFE ON SOUTH HILL STREET

Mulberries, Cherries, and Apples

Living on South Hill Street was almost as good as living on Grandpa Graham's farm. If you walked down the South Hill Street and crossed Curtis Street, South Hill Street then went straight downhill to Dodge Street. Dodge Street was Dubuque's main east-west highway that went straight east to the river bridge across the Mississippi. There were cement steps leading down to Dodge Street. They had a nice rail on them and were easy to walk. When Tom or I wanted to walk to Grandpa Graham's or Grandpa Schiltz's house, all we had to do was cross Dodge Street, walk up the hill on the other side and it led straight to their houses.

The reason that Tom and I spent time on the hill to Dodge Street had nothing to do with the cement steps. The whole east side of the hill had mulberry trees, one after the other almost all the way down the hill. Tom, Jim Sievers and I would climb the mulberry trees maybe once a day. We would sit in the tree and eat as many mulberries as we wanted. While we were eating, our new cocker spaniel dog we called Spunk chased chipmunks, or anything else on four legs, until we were finished eating.

If we got tired of eating mulberries, we could always eat cherries. The Loenbergs lived on South Hill Street directly across from 135 South Hill Street on the other side of York Street. They were really nice people and good neighbors. They had a big cherry tree in their backyard and told Tom and me that we could eat some whenever we wanted to. We both liked cherries and had some at least once or twice a week. Then there was Doc McQuillen, an animal doctor, who lived five houses up on South Hill Street on our side of the street. Doc had a beautiful apple tree in his backyard. Mrs. McQuillen was a nice lady. Whenever Tom or I delivered papers or collected for *The Telegraph Herald* newspaper, Mrs. McQuillen always gave us an apple. We never forgot to thank her.

Racing Neighborhood Cats with Brother Tom and Jim Sievers on York Street

All while Tom and I were growing up we lived at 135 South Hill Street. Our house was on the corner of South Hill Street and York Street. Our cousins Mary Ceil, Martha and Jeannie Schiltz lived on York Street on the east side of South Hill Street. Our house was on the west side of South Hill Street. When we first moved there the only garage on our property was in our backyard and faced York Street. The garage had a double door that opened to York Street but it was only big enough for an old Model-A car. Tom and I could play in the garage where Dad stored some things in it. It wasn't big enough to use it for anything else. There was a big tree up near the southeast corner of the garage and York Street that provided shade for the garage.

Jim Sievers spent a lot of time with Tom and me. He was Tom's classmate at Saint Columbkille's grade school. Our dog Spunk got his name because he spent all day chasing neighbor cats. It seemed like everyone had a cat except Jim Sievers and Bobby Rudzianski, who lived on the Northwest corner of South Hill and Curtis Street, and Tom and I. There were cats in our yard all day long. Some came in the backyard. Some crossed South Hill Street from Ralph Teeling's front yard into our front yard. Some came from the other side of York Street. There were cats everywhere!

What amazed us about the cats was how fast they were. Spunk would appear to be gaining on them and they would put it into the second gear and just fly away. We all got to thinking and wondering how fast cats could be. We decided to find out. The first thing we did was catch a couple of cats. This was not hard to do. All we did was put out a plate of milk and grabbed them when they drank it. We tried holding them down on the pavement of York Street and then yell at them when we let them go. All they did was run a few feet and then walk away.

We tried several other experiments and finally figured out how to make cats run as fast as they were able to run. It really was quite simple. All we had to do was take a little rope or string and tie it really tight around their tail. Then just let the cat go. When we did the cat streaked straight down York Street away from the garage. We were all happy with our scientific discovery. The next day we tried and were successful at catching three cats.

We each lined our tail-tied cats up in the middle of York Street, pointed them west away from the garage and on a signal let them go. Instead of running straight west down York Street again, each cat ran in a separate direction. One even ran up the tree next to the garage. There it was at the top of the tree hanging onto the little tiny branches. What we learned was that Spunk would do what he was told but we could never count on a cat.

ALMOST   TROUBLE   WITH   THE   LAW

South Hill Street Apple Raid

The only neighbors that were not really nice or generous with their apple tree were the Blades. The Blades lived right next to Mr. and Mrs. McQuillen. Whenever Tom and I collected money from the Blades for our newspaper delivery for the *Telegraph Herald*, they always complained about us not putting the paper exactly where they wanted it. They continually asked us why we were so late in delivering the paper. We did not know that there was an exact time required for delivery. We never dillydallied when we delivered papers. Mom said that we had to be courteous to all the people we delivered papers to. So we always apologized and told him that we would try to do better. The Blades' complaining went on for almost a year. Finally Tom and I had had enough.

The Blades had a beautifully trimmed and maintained apple tree right in the middle of their backyard. The tree itself was surrounded by beautifully mowed green grass. Their driveway to their garage started at York Street. Their backyard went up to the house and its basement-level garage. The backyard itself was always illuminated by two high-powered searchlights, one of which was directly pointed at the apple tree.

Tom and I asked Mom if she would dye two of the sheets from our bunk beds green. Sure enough when Tom and I got back from school we saw that Mom had dyed both the sheets green. The problem was that they were both a pukey yellow green. They were not the dark green that we needed. So I thanked Mom for doing it and asked her if she would dye them again so that they would be a dark green. She never asked us why we wanted them dyed again and said she would do it.

The next day when we got home, Tom and I pulled the sheets out of the washing machine. I looked at Tom and Tom looked at me. We both yelled: "PERFECT!" We now had the most important tool to implement our plan. We started checking for backup and support resources. We needed two things in order to implement our plan. The first was strong cloth sacks. This was easy enough to find at Grandpa Graham's farm. All we had to do was to bring back two feed sacks that Uncle Charlie used to mix feed for the horses and the cows. The second resource was the army pup tent that Dad bought for us so that we could sleep outside at the farm. The pup tent was three and a half feet above the ground, dark green and had plenty of room for our big army sleeping bags.

Finally, we had everything we needed to implement our plan to crawl up the Blades' grassed search-lighted backyard and steal some apples. We put the tent up in our backyard next to the garage where it could not be seen from our house and faced the tent entrance to York Street. After it got real dark that night, we told Mom and Dad we were going to sleep in the tent. We told one another that the only way this was going to work was for us to keep the green sheets over us at all times as we very slowly crawled up the Blades' backyard to the base of the apple tree. We crossed York Street covered in the sheets and started our crawl to the apple tree. I kept telling Tom to slow down, and he did.

When we got to the base of the apple tree, we crawled up the York Street side into the tree itself. It was kind of hard to hang on to the limbs and keep hold of the gunnysacks while at the same time you were picking the apples. We had both agreed that we would not fill the gunnysacks because they would be too heavy. I crawled down the tree, covered myself with the sheet, and started crawling toward our tent. You couldn't see the tent from the apple tree because it was in the shadow of the garage. When I got about halfway out of the yard, I heard Tom yell and fall to the ground. He quickly collected himself, put some apples back into his sack, put the sheet over him and ran out of their yard. When Tom got halfway to York Street, the Blades also turned on their back porch lights and started yelling.

Tom ran into the darkness by our garage and we both got into the tent. Our sleeping bags were for grown-ups, so there was plenty of room in the back of the sleeping bags to hide the sheets, apples and the gunnysacks. We thought it would be a good idea if we just stayed there and pretended to sleep.

Half an hour later, we heard a car pull up to our house and park on York Street. Whoever was in it walked down York Street past the garage to our tent, shined a light inside and saw Tom and I both sleeping. We later learned that this person was the police chief, Mr. O'Brien. We knew him because we saw him once in a while at church. Anyway, time went on and on and on. Maybe after about an hour someone came out of our house, got into the car and left. After a while, Tom and I both fell asleep.

We didn't wake up until eight o'clock or so. We woke to the growl of a chainsaw. We peeked out of the tent and saw Mr. Blades cutting down the apple tree. We got to talking about that and decided that Mr. and Mrs. Blades would rather cut down their apple tree than give an apple to anyone, especially to us. That brought a satisfying smile to our faces. Even so, the more we thought about it, the more we both figured we had to tell this to Msgr. Dunn next week when we went to confession.

It Is "Dung," Not "Shit"

Tom and I thought that the Blades issue was over. We were wrong. All of this happened on Saturday. When Monday came, the *Telegraph Herald* newspaper called Mom and she told us that the Blades had canceled their newspaper subscription. I thought this was a good thing in some ways. We gave this a little more thought and came up with a new idea when we found out that the Blades had said all kinds of bad things about Tom and me to the paper.

We knew that we could not cuss at them and could not let the air out of their car's tires. We thought and thought on what we could do to let the Blades know how we appreciated their support on the paper route. Finally, we got the best idea there ever was!

We knew it did not make any difference to the *Telegraph Herald* because all of our customers were really happy with how we delivered the paper. A lot of them even gave us a tip when we collected the fees. The paper even wanted us to make our route bigger so that we could include more people. We told him that we had enough and that there were other things we wanted to be able to do. I think it was Tom who came up with the idea. At least now that I think about it, I want to blame Tom for it. ☺

The idea went something like this. We would get one of Mom's old, big cookie sheets. We needed something that was eighteen inches wide, maybe two feet long and an inch deep. We planned to fill that tray with an inch of the worst smelling shit we could find and put it in front of the Blades' front door so when they opened the door they could step in it and enjoy it.

We asked Mom if we could have one of her old cookie sheets. It was the perfect size. That was the easy part. Mom agreed to let us have it. She did not ask us what we wanted to use it for. When we went to Grandma and Grandpa Graham's farm on weekends, Tom and I filled coffee cans and other cans with pig shit, horse shit, cow shit, chicken shit and donkey shit. I feel bad about using the word *"shit."* Mom told us it was a word that we should never use. She would punish us if we used it. The right word was *"dung."*

We covered the tops of the full cans and put them in Dad's trunk where nobody knew they were there. When we got home we put all of the dung in the garage. The next day we started mixing it up to see what combination was the worst possible smelling. We even added our dog Spunk's dung to the mix. It was amazing to see what worked and what didn't work. Finally, we came up with the perfect mix.

The problem was how to get the dung and cookie sheet up to the Blades' front door without spilling the special mix on us. We solved the problem by Tom carrying the empty cookie sheet. I got one of Dad's old, empty, gallon paint cans from the basement with a lid on it. We filled the paint can with the perfect mix. The next night it was really dark. I carried the perfect mix in the paint can, and Tom the cookie sheet. When we got on their front porch, we put it together right under the Blades' front door, rang the doorbell and ran. We heard the door open and only one word was said. It was "S-H-I-I-I-I-I-T!" I don't remember how I got back home I was laughing so hard. Tom and I agreed never to talk about this again. Thank God Mom never asked what happened to her old cookie sheet.

After we thought about it, we decided it was not necessary to tell Monsignor Dunn about the dung.

THE YORK STREET THEATER AND CASINO

There were a lot of kids in our neighborhood. Some lived on Curtis Street, South Hill Street and some on York Street. Everybody had friends who lived a little farther away. Our Mom did a lot of acting when she was in Clark College. Mom's Clark College school yearbook has pictures of her when she was all dressed up playing roles in plays. One day Mom suggested that Tom and I consider putting on a South Hill Street play in the Model-A garage. When we looked at what was in the garage and how big it was, we thought that Mom was right.

Tom and I collected newspapers from all over the neighborhood to turn in for money. I do not remember what they were being collected for. We had bound the papers into bundles about two feet thick. They were bound with extra twine we got from Grandpa Graham's farm. There must've been forty bundles in the garage. All we had to do was line the bundles up in a row and everybody would have seats. We cleared the back of the garage and hung a sheet near the back where our players could change their clothes or wait till their lines had to be said it would all work.

We asked Mom if she knew of a play we could practice and give. She did and gave us something from Shakespeare. I don't remember what it was specifically, but it was eight pages long and required two boys and maybe three girls to do the parts. Mom suggested that we use our cousins Mary Ceil, Martha and Jeanie Schiltz. They lived only a couple of houses away from us on York Street on the east side of South Hill Street. Tom and I went over to their house and asked our cousins if they wanted to be in the play with us. They thought about it and the next day said they did. Mom got us copies of the play and we gave a copy to everyone. Practice time started the next day with Tom, me, and the three girls. We walked through our parts and tried to say the words correctly and got an idea of what was going on as clearly as we could.

The girls had trouble either wanting to or doing what the play called for. Finally, by the second day, we all got it right. Or at least I thought we did. Our garage theater was ready, and the only thing we had to do was decide on a backup or secondary activity to keep people busy. We knew that the play would only take fifteen or twenty minutes. This was a time when the radio, TV and newspapers were all talking about the evils of gambling. We didn't see any big deal in gambling. So we decided to make a spinning wheel and a beanbag throwing board where people could win some money by playing games for the rest of the afternoon.

Making the beanbag throw board was easy. Grandpa Schiltz's contractor materials shed was practically in our backyard. It was located immediately west of our next-door neighbor at 125 South Hill Street. Grandpa had many partially used pieces of plywood, and all I had to do was pick two that were two feet wide and four feet long. I drew the circle at the top of the boards for the beanbag hole, cut the hole with my dad's small hole cutting hand saw, sanded the edges of the hole and painted the boards white. A couple of hinges under the boards attached to a standup piece of plywood made the whole thing solid.

The spinning wheel was a lot harder. I had to make a perfect circle on the outside edge of the wheel and the second circle an inch inside the first circle and then drill a hole for the wheel to spin on. We had to use the perfect center point of the board to balance it on the rod that the board would spin on. After that was done, I had to place dowels exactly the same distance apart all around the outside of the spinning wheel. I explained what I was trying to do to Grandpa Schiltz. He and I made the perfect spinning wheel. Grandpa showed me how to balance the wheel and how to keep it all oiled so the wheel spun smoothly at the same speed.

All while this was going on Tom, Mary Ceil, Jeannie, Martha, and I were also trying to figure out how to act in the play. This was a frustrating process for me. Every time I had an idea on how to say something in the play, or what it meant, one of the girls had a different idea. Little by little and line by line, we worked through all of these how to say it and how to do it issues.

Finally, I thought we were ready to advertise and invite the neighbors to our play. Tom and I wrote up a flyer advertising both the play and players and the gambling day. Mom decorated the flyer with a drawing of the players in costume and helped us figure out what our costumes would be. Dad copied the flyers. Tom and I and the girls distributed them all over the neighborhood.

On the flyer we told everyone to bring a dollar so they could play the games. It assured that everyone who came could take their winnings home with them. We also told everyone that cookies would be served after the festivities. The whole neighborhood showed up. There must have been fifty kids there. Everybody came alone. It was just us kids, no parents.

The first event on the schedule was the play. We had room for forty people, but not fifty. Some had to stand against the walls or just inside the garage doors. I really don't know what happened when we introduced ourselves and started the play. It was like the girls had completely rewritten what we had agreed to do. Their lines came out different and they asked questions instead of going on with the script. Tom and I looked at one another and we knew there was nothing we could do except to play along and try to figure out how to respond. There was no way of knowing what was coming next. Our confusion must have been funny because everybody in the audience started to laugh at it. Line by line we finally got through the whole thing and most everybody applauded.

After the day was over, Tom and I got to talking about what happened in the play and why it happened. We finally concluded that the answer to our questions was one word, GIRLS. In some ways the GIRLS were like cats. You never knew what they were going to do next. At the same time we both realized that at some time in their lives they must change. We couldn't figure out any other way to explain how they could end up being like our Mom who always loved us and helped us. That was the last time we invited the Schiltz girls to play. After that, we only saw them at church and at family get-togethers. They kind of went their way, and Tom and I went our way.

The spinning wheel and the beanbag games lasted twice as long as we figured they would. We set the beanbag game up so that everyone played against one another for a championship of five dollars. Four or five kids lost half of their entry dollar by losing their first game. The same thing happened on the second, third, fourth, and fifth rounds. It took almost two hours before the last two players were identified. At this point, half the kids started cheering for one of the final winners. The other half cheered for the other final winner.

As this was going on, I was taking people's bets on the spinning wheel. The kids bet a quarter and got five spins of the wheel. If we added all the places where the wheel stopped and it came up to five dollars they would win a dollar. I did the spinning to assure that every spin was at the same speed and everyone had the same chance. A couple of kids won two or three dollars. Most everybody lost their dollar even though they bet a quarter at a time. I felt sorry for our friend Bobby Rudzianski. Bobby brought two dollars, not just one, and had lost them both. So I put my dollar down for him and spun the wheel.

There was one stop on the entire wheel that had "Five Dollars" on it and the wheel stopped right there! I gave Bobby the five dollars he won. It was a good thing that Bobby and I were the only ones at the wheel when that happened. They might have thought that somehow the wheel was fixed, but it wasn't. At the time I blamed Bobby's winnings on God doing the right thing. You know it could have been!

SOUTH HILL RASCALS' FIRST FLIGHT

This was a magic summer. We built a lot of things and didn't believe there was anything we could not do. One day on TV, they were showing a one-man hang glider that Michelangelo designed hundreds of years ago but never tested. Tom and I were fascinated by the design. We got copies of it from the library. It didn't seem all that hard. The flyer put his arms through two straps close to his shoulder in order to put the long wings on his back. There were handholds on both wings that could be used to adjust the flight. Tom and I searched through Grandpa Schiltz's materials barn looking for light and strong wood that we could make the wing framework out of.

It took us a day to find long pieces of thin oak that was really strong and could also be bent without breaking. We set up a piece of plywood on sawhorses in the Model-A garage and got the strongest wood glue we knew of. There were a couple of joints in the back where the two wings connected that we had to use glue and canvas on in order to make it strong enough and still be movable or flexible with our arms. I don't remember where Mom got the silk. We used silk to cover both wings. It took a couple of weeks to put it all together. Dad and Grandpa Schiltz gave us some suggestions on how it all was supposed to work.

The side yard between our house and our neighbors Ines and Earl Dalton and their young daughters at 125 South Hill St. dropped off six feet to the lower-level backyard. Tom and I both experimented with running down the yard and trying to fly with the wings on. The wings really worked. When we hit the ground, we hit softly. We kept practicing for a couple of days. It was fun and everybody in the neighborhood watched us. The real question was where could we test the wings to see how well they really worked? We finally decided that Bobby Rudzianski's, at that time, flat-roofed garage was the best place. The garage itself was twelve feet high and the backyard dropped off another eight feet into the Knornschilds' grassed backyard. That gave us twenty feet of height to fly in. We could get a good head start by running across the flat-roofed garage.

We both wanted the other one to be the test pilot. We thought about it for a while and then observed that Bobby was fifteen pounds lighter than we were. So we decided that he would be the best test pilot. The next day when everybody was together, including Bobby, Tom and I argued with one another, both wanting to be the test pilot. We explained to everyone there how much fun it would be and why we wanted to do it. The argument went on for ten minutes. Finally, Bobby volunteered to be the test pilot in order to prevent Tom and me from fighting one another over it. We agreed and put the wings on Bobby. The wings fit him and we went through several test runs in our yard. Bobby seemed to understand how it all worked and actually did a little gliding for five feet or so.

That afternoon Bobby got up on his flat-roofed garage. After a couple of practice runs, he dove full speed off of the garage. The wings held him up so he missed the rock wall at the end of his lot and landed almost safely in the Knornschilds' backyard. We tried but we couldn't think of any other safe place to try the wings. We ultimately forgot about them.

OUR WONDERFUL GROWING-UP TIMES

Until now, it sounds like Tom and I always got along well. This was not always the case. At night when we went to bed I slept on the top bunk. I will never know why Tom thought it was funny to wait until I fell asleep and then push me out of the top bunk so I fell

47

on the floor. He would then wait for a night and do it again. After a couple of times, Dad had enough of it. He came up to our bedroom, bent us over our toy box and spanked us. Tom waited a couple of days and then did it again. Of course, Dad would spank us again. The next time, I was ready for Tom. Instead of falling on my face, I fell on my feet and raced to the bedroom door so Tom could not get away.

I took my time and forced him into a corner where I could get a good shot at his head. I hit him as hard as I could, and he fell to the floor. In five minutes he had a big lump on the side of his head. Dad came into the bedroom. I really got it that day. Both Mom and Dad really sympathized with Tom. I told them that my hand hurt but they ignored me. Two days later, Mom took me to the doctor. He told her that I had broken my hand. They sat us down together and made us both promise not to fight anymore unless it was necessary to protect one another. We both promised we would. As it turned out, it was a good thing that we promised.

These were wonderful summers for Tom and me. The *Telegraph Herald* paper route required us to deliver one hundred papers every day to everyone who lived on South Hill Street, Grandview Street, and Bradley Street. Our route spanned from the fire station on the south across from Sullivan's grocery store to three blocks north of South Hill Street on Grandview. It included the full length of Bradley Street from the north end all the way to the golf course parking lot on the south end.

The Dubuque Golf and Country Club Golf Course

The Dubuque Golf and Country Club golf course was particularly meaningful to Tom and me. This was true all through grade school, both before and after we carried papers for the Dubuque *Telegraph Herald*. Once a week, or so, we would walk west across the golf course, down the Creek Valley up to Freemont Street.

We would cross Catfish Creek on Freemont Street and walk over the two high hills to Grandpa Graham's farm on Cedar Cross Road. Every time we walked across the golf course, we saw people golfing, got a good look at the greens and the fairways, collected lost balls, and waved to people who were playing as we walked by.

I remember one time we saw an area around a green that was full of ground squirrel holes. We noticed there was a water faucet and a long water hose nearby. Tom and I put two and two together and remembered that the golf course paid a dollar for every dead ground squirrel. That afternoon Tom and I got an idea. We went home and got Dad's wood-handled driver golf club and a bucket full of rags. When we got back to the golf course we stuffed rags into the eight or nine ground squirrel holes. Then Tom turned on the water and ran it into the holes while I waited at the only open hole with the driver. As the ground squirrels came up out of the hole, I wacked them with the driver. I think we got nine ground squirrels. We took them up to the clubhouse and they put nine dollars into our pockets!

Rabbit and Squirrel Trapping

In our walks across the golf course on our way to Grandpa's Graham's farm, when I was in the fifth grade, Tom and I noticed that west of the golf course for a mile or so there was a small creek area that was full of rabbits and squirrels on all sides of the creek. A month earlier, after delivering the newspapers, we caught a rabbit in our backyard. We asked Mom if she would cook it for us. She did. It was really good! Mom sure knew what she was doing! Then we came up with a plan. We figured that if we had four or five wooden box traps, we could catch enough rabbits so that we could have rabbit once a week.

We asked Dad how to build a rabbit trap with a front door that closed the box when the door slid down. It was easy. In a week we had four box traps made. We cut an apple in half with the juicy part upward and stuck it on the bait stick at the far end inside of the box trap. We put the traps in our wagon and went to the creek. We found four spots that were hidden behind bushes so that people walking by could not see them. The next day after delivering papers we walked out to check the traps, and sure enough we had our first rabbit. We rebaited the trap and took the rabbit home. Dad showed us how to clean it so Mom could cook it. We were right: rabbit is REAL good.

Eventually, we made two more box traps and had to substitute our sled for the wagon when checking the traps after a snow. For Christmas that year, Mom and Dad bought us three small steel traps. The steel traps were harder to find a good place for. Tom found a big, flat rock that stuck up on the ground leaning over on one side so that there was a protected area under the rock. For a week the steel traps caught nothing, so we changed the bait to bacon. The first day after we used bacon Tom caught a skunk. We were not about to get close enough to it to get sprayed. Dad had a 22 rifle. We snuck it out of the house and shot the skunk with it. I think Tom washed that steel trap four times. He used soap and water and even gasoline before he caught anything else with it. That was the last skunk we caught in a trap before we started to catch squirrels. As far as we were concerned, squirrel was good too. Mom would cook either rabbit or squirrel. We always had a backup for the next meal in the freezer down in the basement. Then one day Tom and I made a really bad mistake when we caught a squirrel in a box trap. We brought the trap home, put it in the basement and went to school without killing and skinning the squirrel.

The squirrel chewed its way out of the wood box trap. Sometime in the afternoon when Tom and I got back from school, we heard Mom screaming in the basement. We ran down to the basement and Mom was standing in the corner of the basement with her back to the wall next to the washing machine. Mom was rubbing her hair with her hands. We ran to her, put our arms around her and told her everything was all right. She acted like she didn't, or couldn't, hear us. We led her upstairs to the kitchen and sat her down on a chair. On the way up from the stairs, we both knew what the problem was, as the squirrel was running free in the basement.

We went downstairs again, got our tennis rackets, and went after the squirrel. It was really fast. We finally cornered it and got it. We skinned the squirrel, wrapped it, and put it into the freezer with all the other wild meats. When we went upstairs, Mom was feeling better. We told her that we loved her and held her for a minute or two. She seemed to be okay. We decided that we were going to stop our trapping so nothing like this could ever happen again. We didn't waste anything that we had in the freezer but we brought the traps home and put them in the Model-A garage. For a month or so when we woke up, one of the first things we did was to tell Mom that we loved her. This was not something she did not already know but we wanted her to hear it anyway.

GRAHAM BACKYARD FREEDOM SHACKS

Our First Shack

That summer and fall at South Hill Street was wonderful. It didn't take long for Tom and me to be tired of using Dad's army tent to sleep outdoors in our backyard. We got to thinking about how nice it would be if we had a real shack with a roof on it and maybe a window and a door so we could close it to keep mosquitoes out. We figured we could always sleep in our sleeping bags, or on them, if it got too hot. Our backyard was not totally dark because there was some light from the street light at the corner of South Hill Street and York Street. We figured we could always carry a flashlight if we needed it.

The next time Grandpa Schiltz came to get stuff from his materials barn behind 125 South Hill Street. Tom and I talked to him. He didn't see any problem with what we planned to do. He showed us where there was reused or partly used plywood and miscellaneous two by fours and boards we could use to build our first shack. Grandpa talked to us and kind of gave us an idea of how to build the sides and how to put a roof on the shack. Then he gave us a few nails. Tom and I got Dad's saw and hammer from the basement and started to build our first shack.

It took us a couple days to finish it. The hard part was making the door and the window fit. We had to rebuild the front side of the shack to refit the window to make the door work. The next day, after we had finished the shack, Grandpa Schiltz came by to look at it. He thought we had done a good job for our first shack! Grandpa gave us some ideas on what to do when we built our next one. We slept in the shack for a week or two and then got tired of crawling around on our knees. It wasn't all that comfortable even to sit in.

Neighborhood Defense

We had no sooner finished our first shack when we found out that Bob Weitert, who lived on the north side of Curtis Street, had a shack. It was located in his backyard next to the rock cliff that fell down to Dodge Street. Bob Weitert was a year older than me, and he tended to think that he owned the world. The more that Tom and I thought about it, the more we realized we had to rebuild our shack because it was totally vulnerable to attack from every side except the side that faced our house.

Our shack had to be tall enough so that we could stand up in it and stick a BB gun out any side. We needed a tower that was four or five feet above the roof of the shack. The tower would give us a way to hit any attackers by shooting down at them even when we were still a long way away from the shack. Attackers would not know there was anyone in the tower until it was too late because it was dark. Tom and I drew up the plans for our shack and tore apart the old one for material. To get air through the shack, we made small open windows on the back and sides. We covered the openings with a double layer of fly or mosquito wire. That way, the wire would be strong enough to keep BBs from coming into the shack. It took two weeks for us to build the new shack. We finally figured out that all we had to do to make the tower was to put a hole in the middle of the roof so we could stand up inside the tower on a small step ladder.

It didn't take long for Bob Weitert's gang to find out that we had our new shack. As soon as Tom and I finished the shack we started sleeping in it. One night when Joe Meyer, a friend of ours who lived up South Hill Street, was sleeping with us, our dog Spunk started to bark. We knew that AN ATTACK was on! I took my BB gun, stood on the small step ladder and looked in every direction. Joe Meyer kept Spunk quiet as Tom started looking out of the other sides of the shack. The first thing we did was turn off our flashlight to help us see better in the dark. It didn't take long and I could see two people crawling up in the grass in the Daltons' backyard. They were still too far away. I remembered that Dad told us if we ever hit someone in the head with our BB guns, we could really hurt them. If that happened we would not only lose our BB guns but also every other privilege he could think of. Knowing this created a practical problem.

We could not shoot at them when they were far away crawling on the ground because we were likely to get them in the head. I was a good shot. I knew I could hit them while they were still in the neighbor's yard but I could not take the shot. In some ways it was better that I had to wait until they got closer. Once they crawled into our yard it was a perfect shot. I hit both of them. They didn't say much until after I hit them the second time. They both jumped up, yelled and ran out of our yard. I think Tom and I and Joe Meyer must have laughed for ten minutes. Tom was a little unhappy because he didn't get a chance to even take a shot. We talked and talked about how good our shack was and finally went to sleep late at night. We decided there really wasn't any reason to tell Mom or Dad what happened.

Joe Meyer's Two-Hour Shack

There are two other shack stories that I will NEVER forget. A couple weeks later, Joe Meyer asked Tom and me if we would help him build a shack in his backyard. We, of course, said that we would. We got some building materials and brought it up to his house. All Joe wanted was a long enough shack with room for two people to sleep in it. This was no big deal. We had it built without the door in the front in a couple of hours. After we finished we sat down and had a bottle of pop. As we talked, Tom told Joe Meyer that maybe someday he would like to come up and sleep in Joe's shack with him. After Tom said that, Joe told Tom that this was *his* shack and that neither Tom nor I would be invited to sleep in the shack since we had our own shack.

Neither Tom nor I said anything. We just finished our pop and went home. As soon as we got home we went to Grandpa Schiltz's materials shed and got two long poles. Both poles were longer than Joe Meyer's shack. When we got to Joe's shack we stuck the poles under the roof so they stuck out at both the front and in the back. Tom and I lifted opposite ends of the shack on a cross two-by-four board under the long poles on our shoulders. We both carried the shack down South Hill Street to our house. As we got out into the street, Mrs. Meyers came out of her house and yelled at us. Once we got the shack to our house. It took us five minutes to completely disassemble Joe's shack and put the material back in Grandpa's shed. The police never showed up, but we stopped being friends with Joe Meyer for a while.

Sherman Mayne's Shack on Stilts

Maybe the funniest story about a shack is the Sherman Mayne shack story. Sherman was a year older than me. He lived in a house on Grandview Avenue just two doors south of the entrance to South Hill Street. He didn't have much backyard because twenty feet east of his house the backyard dropped almost straight down six or eight feet and leveled off from there. That was then. Today all the lower land east of Sherman's house is built up with houses. Sherman dug in two old half telephone poles standing straight up and away from the drop off. He added two more short old telephone poles halfway between the edge of the bank and the first two telephone poles. He tied all the poles together and to the bank with two long two by four boards and built a platform on top of the two by four boards. On this platform he built a shack that was tall enough to walk in. It had big windows on three sides overlooking the lower flat land. That gave him a level walkway from his backyard out to his new shack that he built on the telephone pole stilts.

Sherman was a genius! He told everyone, including all of our friends, that his shack was 100 percent safe and could not be successfully attacked. All of our friends had to listen to Sherman simply because they lived near him. Sherman told everyone of the design superiority his shack had. He blamed the Graham shack deficiencies on our not being all that smart or skillful. After a couple of weeks of hearing all of this, Tom and I decided that we would test his theory that he could not be successfully attacked because of his foolproof design.

The more Tom and I thought about it, we realized that in order to prove that his shack could be successfully attacked we had to have protection from Sherman's BB guns. That was because the only way we could get near his shack was to approach it in the open field. This was not the worst problem that we ever solved. The first thing we did was build wooden shields on two sides of our big four-wheeled wagon and Bobby Rudzianski's big four-wheeled wagon. That was not hard to do. All we had to do was screw plywood to the front and the left side of the wagon right through the metal. For Tom's wagon, we screwed plywood to the front and the right side of his wagon so that we could attack their shack from both sides at the same time. We were sure that Sherman had BB guns, but he was a stationary target and we could be continually moving. Sherman had windows on all three sides of his shack. The windows were big enough and low enough so we could shoot and not hit anyone in the head.

We made sure that we had plenty of BBs, put our army helmets on and headed for Sherman's shack. When we got there we were lucky because Sherman had three or four people with him. They would be witnesses to what happened. I approached the shack on its door side so I could keep people from running out and up the wooden walk. If they got away, they could attack us from our unprotected sides. Tom approached from the other side. Sherman saw us coming and started shooting at us before we got close enough to be really sure of our shots. It wasn't long after Tom and I started shooting that we could hear people in the shack yelling, then whining as they got hit.

This went on for almost a half an hour until people started running away from the shack toward Sherman's house, knowing they were going to be hit. Soon Sherman was alone. After he got hit a couple more times, he ran out of the shack screaming and fell straight down to the ground. Tom and I looked at each other. We didn't think it was in our best interest to stick around so we ran in different directions. While Sherman was chasing me, Tom brought both of the wagons back to our house. He did not catch me but he came close until I was sure that Tom had the wagons back home. Sherman was really mad! The next day, Sherman took his shack apart and never built another one.

John Flynn's Impregnable Shack on Top of Curtis Street Cliffs

Everything was quiet in the shack world until the end of summer when everybody was thinking about going back to school. When Jim Sievers, Joe Meyers and some of our other buddies got together, we all became aware that John Flynn had built a shack on top of the cliff a couple of houses east of South Hill Street where it went downhill to Dodge Street. The word was that John Flynn and two of his friends had built the perfect shack. The reason it was perfect was because they had built their shack around four old sawed off telephone poles one for each corner. They buried each pole three feet into the ground and built their shack around them. Tom and I didn't have much to do with John Flynn. He was three or four years older than I was and he just hung around with different people. We all lived basically in the same neighborhood. Everything that John and his buddies said became public knowledge.

Their message was that the Flynn shack was superior because of their obvious advanced skill and knowledge. Looking back at it now, they may have been right. When John grew up he started Flynn Construction Company and built highways and everything else in Iowa and Illinois for years. John even ended up with a cottage at Fentress Lake on the Illinois side of the Mississippi River four or five cottages north of the Graham family cottage. This big neighborhood conversation went on for about a week. Finally, Tom and I had had enough. At the same time, we realized that if we did anything to that shack, and people knew who did it, we could lose our shack to a raid.

Tom and I had a plan. We would use the green bunk bed sheets to crawl up to their shack from South Hill Street without being seen. Grandpa Schiltz showed us how to sharpen his crosscut handsaws. We sharpened them as much as we could. The saws were perfect. The problem was not sneaking up on their shack. Nor was it in cutting the telephone poles off at the ground. All we had to do to accomplish that was to take it slow and be as quiet as we could. The problem was how to escape so that no one knew who did it. This took some real scouting. The cliff was fifty or sixty feet high. We figured that if we ran either east or west on the high side of the cliff someone would see us and we would be caught. The only way that could work was for us to go straight down the cliff, split up and run in different directions. It took us a couple of hours to find two separate ways to climb up and down the cliff, where we could do it quickly and quietly.

Now that our plan was complete, we waited for a quiet evening, put on our sheets and crawled to the shack. The problem was worse than we had anticipated. John Flynn, his north side of Curtis Street neighbor Bob Weitert, and three or four others were in Bob Weitert's backyard. They were only half a football field away playing some kind of a card game. It was easy to keep the sheets over us when we were cutting the poles. However, the saws made too much noise unless we pushed them *really* slowly. It took us much longer to cut all four telephone poles than we thought it would.

Once all the poles were cut, we had to stand up—covered in the sheets   in front of the shack and push it up so that it would fall over the cliff. It was heavier than we thought it would be and it took two or three tries. When we began to succeed in pushing the shack over the cliff it started creaking and cracking. It made a huge noise when it fell down the cliff. Tom and I slung the saws and sheets over our backs and raced down the cliff. Tom went west, I went east, and we didn't go home for two hours. It worked! No one saw us and no one knew who did it. All we heard was some yelling as we ran away.

Sixty years later, I was talking to John Flynn after the Frentress Lake Fourth of July parade. I asked him if he ever found out who dumped their shack down the cliff. He looked at me, smiled and said: "I should have known."

CHAPTER 2—ST. COLUMBKILLE'S GRADE SCHOOL

Sister Mary (Agony) Agatha—The Beginning

My brothers Tom, Joe, John, and I all went to grade school at Saint Columbkille's Parish in Dubuque. The school was easy to get to, as it was located on Rush Street a little more than a mile away from South Hill Street where we lived. The school had a kindergarten and classes through and including eighth grade. When Tom and I were at Saint Columbkille, the principal of the school was Msgr. Joseph Dunn. All of the teachers were sisters, or nuns who dressed in their black-and-white habits. Grade school was more or less uneventful for me until fifth grade. I don't mean that it wasn't fun or that we didn't learn anything. Other chapters of this book testify to the fact that we did. Nor do I mean that I did not appreciate the Saint Columbkille grade school. I enjoyed every class in it. Maybe because I did, fifth grade was special.

Sister Mary Agatha was my teacher in the fifth grade. These earlier grades did not always mean much from a character-building point of view. It wasn't that I didn't have good grades. Everybody had good grades because the subject matter wasn't all that difficult. There was plenty of time to learn it. Learning how to write or spell was no big deal. In these earlier classes, it was just a matter of getting through the day, enjoying recess and then going home to do something that was more fun.

There were three or four guys in my class who were always causing some kind of commotion. They would interrupt things at the right time, or at the wrong time, as the case may be. Or they told the teacher that they just did not understand the question. It seemed like anything that kind of broke up the rhythm of the day was not all bad. Everything changed when I got into Sister Mary Agatha's fifth grade.

The first day I knew something was wrong. The three or four guys who used to break up the class just sat in their desks and said nothing. This was not right. I thought that maybe they were all sick even though having everyone sick at the same time didn't make a lot of sense. This went on for three days. The class as a whole continued to be cordial and business like and made steady progress.

Sister Mary Agatha was nice and was even kind to some of the girls. Then one day halfway through the class she picked up a big, long ruler and quickly walked down an aisle and smacked the poor guy on his unprotected hands. Even though he didn't want to, he yelled. Sister Mary Agatha had seen him throw a wet spit wad at one of the other guys. This was not the end of it. She grabbed him by his ears, pulled him out of his seat, and sat him down on her swivel stool in front of the piano. She started to spin the stool and when his face came around, she slapped it. She did this for three spins. She took him off the stool and told him to go back to his seat. Without another word she went right back to teaching the class. At that point, I remembered what Mom had told me. She said: "Jim, when something good happens to you just take a second and thank God for it." I thanked God that it was not me.

Sister Mary Agatha did not just teach her coursework. She continually asked everybody in the class what they were learning really meant and how we could use it later. Those were new thoughts to me. The more I heard them, the more they made sense to me. I think this was the most important lesson I had ever learned, whether in fifth grade, in high school, in the army or in college. In law school I always asked myself the same question. Once I knew how I could use it and why it was important it was easier to learn.

As I grew older, finished school, and had a family. I sometimes thought of Sister Mary Agatha and wished I had gone back to Saint Columbkille grade school to thank her. Sixty years later my wife, Jane, and I were at the Mount Olivet Cemetery southwest of Dubuque burying a member of our family. We walked up to the high hill part of the cemetery where there was a very large circle of big trees. I think they were oak trees. It was a beautiful spot with the sun shining in the grass inside the circle of trees. We noticed that there were surface stones with names on them in neat rows. I looked down at my feet with Jane standing right next to me and I read: "Sister Mary Agatha." I told Jane this story. We were both amazed and stood there thanking Sister Mary Agatha for all that she had done to help me become who God intended to me to be. Grade school was a lot of fun and I learned a lot of things but maybe none or anything more important than what Sister Mary Agatha taught me those many years ago in fifth grade.

Irene Kringle and Tom's Broken Arm

Tom and I walked to school every day from 135 South Hill Street. One day, Tom was a little bit behind me and he came upon a new girl in school that we later found out was Irene Kringle. Irene was a bigger girl. Tom came up to her when she was slapping a small girl in the face. Tom told Irene to stop doing that. Then Irene made a big mistake. Tom may have been smaller than her but Tom blocked Irene's punch and punched her in the eye with one hand and on the jaw with the other hand. Irene went down and sat on the sidewalk. She looked straight ahead but did not act like she was seeing anything. In a second or two, Irene stood up and watched Tom help the little girl into school.

That first episode between Irene and Tom seemed to change things with Irene, or so we thought. A couple weeks later, Tom had broken his right arm and went to school with his right arm in a cast. As we walked out of school going home, I saw Irene watching Tom. She had seen his cast. Tom headed home and Irene followed him and I followed Irene. Nothing happened until they both got to the first house on York Street east of South Hill Street, which was right in front of Mom's brother's house—Uncle Vern Schiltz.

At that point Irene had caught up to Tom and I started to run toward both of them. As I got near, Irene was on her knees on the ground and Tom was hitting her on the top of her head with his cast. We just left Irene kneeling there and went the rest of the way home. Before we got home we talked about our promise to Dad that we would never hit a girl. We decided that maybe Irene was not really a girl and our promise did not apply to her. That was going to be our answer if Dad found out about it.

Bringing Tom Home Alive—Who Is the Toughest Classmate?

I can't remember what grade it was—maybe the fourth, fifth or sixth grade—when I had my first ethics problem with my dad. Tom's grade-school class was just as big as mine, and he probably had twenty boys in his class just like I did. It all started with an argument between Tom and three or four of his classmates. The classmates told Tom that he had better recognize the biggest kid in his class as the toughest kid in the class. This bothered Tom, and Tom and I talked about it. I told Tom not to worry about it because sooner or later there would be an opportunity and a reason to take the kid on and to teach him a lesson. Tom did not agree with my advice, and he came up with the worst solution I could possibly imagine. His plan was to announce to his class that it was necessary to determine who the toughest boy in the class was, and he would give each of them in opportunity to fight him in the north school parking lot across the street from the church after school. The guys in his class, as a group, told him that they would be happy to oblige.

That afternoon when school was out, all the guys in Tom's class met at the parking lot across from the church. Tom picked out the biggest kid in his class to start with. The big kid was surprised. He never really had a chance. Tom hit him five or six times before he could take a deep breath. There was a lot of talk. But it was the end of that episode and Tom and I walked home. This same scene was repeated the next two days. I began to see that the rest of Tom's classmates were not going to put up with this for much longer. I told Tom he should quit but he refused. When we got home, after dinner, I went into the dining room and talked to Dad. I told him what was going on and that I thought it would be a good idea for Tom to get beat up so he could learn something.

Dad totally disagreed with me. We talked for a LONG time. Dad's instructions were clear. "Jim, you must bring Tom home alive!" He told me that Tom and I were going to make some mistakes in dealing with our neighbors and classmates. I agreed that he was probably right. His point was that he would be very, very disappointed with me if I did not step in to help Tom in any case where he had to fight two or more at the same time. Dad knew that Tom and I knew how to fight together. Dad told me that he would be *very, very, very* disappointed in me if I did not protect Tom.

The next day after school, Tom's class met again at the parking lot and Tom chose the next biggest kid in his class as his next proof of who was the toughest kid in the class. It was a fair fight, which lasted for five or six minutes. The kid hit Tom a couple of times but they were all glancing blows. Tom was quicker and was winning when two other kids stepped forward and acted like they were going to jump into the fight. When I moved up a little they stopped. The fight was over and we went home.

I brought Dad up to date but nothing changed. I warned Tom what was going to happen but he didn't care because he knew that I was obligated to join the fight and help him. That was exactly what happened. All of the rest of his classmates made a move to Tom, and he and I had to start circling in our defense circle move. We smacked three or four and they all gave up. That was the last of Tom's classmate fights. Nobody picked on Tom again. In fact after that his class always stuck together, which paid off later in school football games. The subject never came up at home and I often wondered if Dad knew what happened.

Simpson Street Football Game
Saint Columbkille grade school had a football team for their seventh- and eighth-grade classes. Tom and I would watch the football games that were played on our field and thought that that was really fun. There were several other Catholic grade schools in Dubuque that also had seventh- and eighth-grade football teams. The one that I was most familiar with was the Nativity grade school right across the street from Grandpa Schiltz's house on Nevada Street. Tom and I thought that it would be a good idea to put together street football teams so that we could practice and be better ready when we got to seventh grade. There weren't enough boys in our fifth and sixth grade classes to have any more than one team and a backup squad with three or four extra players.

Mark Stevenson lived over by Grandpa and Grandma's Graham's new house on Simpson Street on the west side of South Freemont Avenue. At the intersection of Fremont Avenue and Simpson Street there was an open area that we figured we could play a football game on. I got together with Jim Sievers, Joe Meyers and six or seven other boys from our class. Mark Stevenson did the same thing in his neighborhood. We finally had enough people for a fifth- and sixth-grade football game. We met after school one day, decided where we were going to play and when we would do it. It was a good thing that we had this early meeting. When I saw that Mark Stevenson had recruited most of his players from his and my sixth grade, I knew that we had to come up with some strategy to overcome Mark's apparent size and speed advantage.

Our team met after school in our backyard. We figured out who was going to be playing on the line and who the two people in the backfield were going to be. Dad helped us by showing us how to position ourselves and how to block players on the other side. It was a combination of timing and getting the correct angle on the other guy before we blocked them. Our father, Joseph Gill Graham, knew what he was talking about. I found out later that Dad was the only person in the history of Columbia College (now Loras College) that had a football game dedicated to him. They called it "Joe Graham Day." Dad even had a nickname. The college called him "Bullet Joe."

I told Dad what I thought our physical problem was going to be. We decided that we should concentrate on learning defense so they did not score, because the first team to score won the game. We practiced for three days after school and had our defense down real good. For defensive purposes, we pulled a third person into the backfield so that we could prevent outside or end around runs.

Tom and I figured out what our offensive surprise was going to be but we didn't tell anybody. On the Saturday we got to Simpson Street and were ready to play the game. Both sides of the field had parents, brothers and sisters to watch the game. We had decided that we would play ten-minute halves. And we would start the offense at the end of the field because the field just wasn't that big. The first team to score won. One of the parents flipped a coin. Mark

Stevenson's team won the flip. They chose offense. The Stevenson team made one first down and then they turned the ball over to us.

In this our first series of plays, Mark Stevenson and his team noticed that Tom had some kind of leg problem and could not run at full speed. He always got to where he needed to be, but he was not necessarily the first person to get there. In our first play, I tried to run off the right side of our line and barely made it two yards. Tom ran around the left side of the line and waved for me to throw the ball to him. There was no way that I was going to throw the ball to Tom because he had two of Stevenson's men right next to him. We huddled up again and tried another run right up the center. Jim Sievers threw a good block. This time, I made it three and a half yards. Tom did the same thing, running off to the left waving for my pass, which never came.

On the third down, we lined up the same way. I faked another run around on our right and stopped and threw the ball as hard as I could to Tom. This time, Tom ran straight down the field under the football and caught it. Instead of coming back to pick up the trophy, Tom just kept on running all the way back to South Hill Street with the football. That was a smart move because Mark Stevenson's whole team was after him and he needed a head start. With Tom on his way home, I picked up the trophy and our team left the football field. The more I thought about what happened the funnier it became. What I didn't realize was how what we just learned was going to pay off when our class became seventh and eighth graders.

God Bless Monsignor Joseph Dunn
One day when I was in the sixth grade, I think, as I got to the front of the school I saw this big, stoutly built new guy beating up one of my classmates. He was a lot bigger than the kid he was

hitting and bigger than me. I never saw him before and told him to leave the kid alone. He was finished with that kid anyway and he turned on me. There was no way I could get away from him. All I could do was to make sure that when he hit me they were glancing blows that didn't do any permanent damage. This went on for a minute or two. I ended up with two, maybe three, cuts on my face, not counting all the unseen bruises. He finally let me go.

I was pissed off that I got so beat up. The first thing that came to my mind was Tom. Tom didn't always know when to keep his mouth shut to stay out of trouble. Sooner or later Tom, as well as others, would be confronted with the same problem I just had with John. Then I got an idea. If Msgr. Dunn was aware of the fact that John Cady was a bully, he could help turn John around and that would help everyone.

Instead of going into school I went right into Msgr. Dunn's office. His secretary came away from her desk, got a wet rag, and started wiping the blood off of my face. Msgr. Dunn watched. When I was cleaned up, he came over and asked me who did it. I told him that I did not know what his name was but I knew where his classroom was. That was good enough for Msgr. Dunn. He and I both walked down the school hall to where John Cady's classroom was. John was sitting in the first row right in front of the nun's desk. I walked straight up to John, stuck my finger on his forehead and said: "He did it." Msgr. Dunn grabbed John by his ears and pulled him out from the desk. The last I saw of the two of them, John Cady was walking in front of Msgr. Dunn down the hall toward his office with Father kicking John Cady in the ass.

At lunchtime, I told Tom what happened and we made a plan. After school I waited for an hour and then for two hours until John finally came out of school. The first thing that John saw when the door closed was me. I did not have to call him girly or anything. He just took off after me as fast as he could go. I ran down Alpine Street a half mile to the corner of Curtis Street where there was a small patch of woods. When I got into the woods I slowed up a little so that John could get closer to me. Halfway through the woods Tom stepped out from behind a tree and hit John in the stomach with a big stick. John went down and had trouble breathing. Tom and I hit him until we couldn't lift our arms anymore. We left him lying there and went home figuring we would not have any more trouble with him.

The next day I took my bike to school. On the way home on Grandview Avenue heading north to our house God told me to look behind me. What I saw was someone who I later learned was Fred Cady, John Cady's older brother. Fred was at full speed on a bicycle and bearing down on me. I asked God for help and flew! When I got home, Tom and I talked. We both knew that neither one of us could take either John or his brother Fred alone. So what we tried to do was to figure out how we could find Fred and explain to him that it was in his best interest to leave us alone. We asked all around our neighborhood where Fred went to school and where he worked or who his friends were. We got a lot of conflicting answers. Fred got the message from the people we talked to. He never bothered us. John got well, came back to school and became our friend. Before we left grade school, John Cady made the difference between winning and losing our football games. But that's another story. In fact, John Cady was later able to help our little brother, Joe, when he was the police chief in East Dubuque across the river.

Almost Boy Scouts—Our Temporary Leader

Mom and Dad thought it would be a good idea if we met and played with a broader cross-section of kids in Dubuque. Tom and

I certainly did not have anything against that idea. We figured any new experiences had to be worthwhile and maybe even fun.

I guess they figured that us taking the bus ride out to the north end of town and learning how to swim in the Dubuque swimming pool or taking the bus downtown to watch a Western movie wasn't culturally broad enough. They knew that in these circumstances we always met interesting people because we talked about that a lot, but apparently that was not enough. Then one day the church's Sunday bulletin had an ad that St. Columbkille was going to establish a Boy Scout troop. The new leader was an older high school boy by the name of John Ahern. Tom and I went to the first meeting where Msgr. Dunn and a couple of other fathers introduced John Ahern as the scout leader. We found out that John Ahern had finished high school and was thinking about joining the army or maybe it was the Marines.

There must have been twelve or fifteen brand-new Boy Scouts. We met for a couple of months at the school and went through "how-to" scout books trying to get ready for our first big camp out. Finally, our campout was scheduled for a beautiful summer weekend. Tom and I could not believe it. The camping was going to be done at Catfish Creek! We just looked at each other but didn't say anything. We all brought our tents. The leader's tent was bigger than ours. You could walk into it standing up. There was room for two or three people in the bigger tent but Mr. Ahern was going to be the only leader at this campout.

I think it was a sunshiny Friday afternoon when everybody gathered at the school and put our tents and cooking gear into a big pickup truck. We all marched to our camping site at Catfish Creek. When we got there everybody was hungry. We set up four separate campfires and tried to make hamburgers for dinner. This first effort did not go very well. Mr. Ahern insisted that every fire be set up exactly the same way with exactly the same number of stones. If the scouts that set up the fireplace didn't do it right he would kick all the stones away and told them to do it again. Tom and I did it right the first time but we looked at one another with funny expressions on our faces as all of this was going on. Then the time came for us to set up the tents. We had been instructed at school to set them up in a perfect circle with twelve feet separating one tent from another and with all the tents around the scout leader's larger tent in the middle.

Mr. Ahern tore down Tom's and my tent and instructed us to pitch it a foot away from where we had originally put it up. Next we had to do calisthenics. No one seemed to be able to do this right. We must have spent a whole hour doing it. Just before it got dark we had a free hour. Tom and I went over to Catfish Creek and sat under a tree next to the creek. The tree had a big limb that actually hung over the creek. Tom and I got an idea. It wasn't a good idea but it was the only thing we could think of to get us out of this mess. We waited until everybody was asleep. Our scout leader's tent light had been out for two hours before we made our move. We did not make any noise when we opened up the front of the scout leader's tent. Tom had his rope and I had my rope. Tom slipped his rope around Mr. Ahern's feet and then Tom helped me get ahold of his one semi loose hand. We figured that he would not give anybody any trouble tomorrow. We didn't count on John's mouth. In some ways, this was an interesting experience. We all learned a lot of cuss words we never knew existed. We got to thinking about what was going to happen when Msgr. Dunn came to the campout tomorrow.

Everybody participated in a group discussion. It was agreed that no one wanted Mr. Ahern to be the scout leader anymore. What we decided was that we had to find a way to embarrass him so that he didn't want to be a scout leader either. Finally, we had enough of his cussing. We double tied his feet together, swung a rope over the tree branch, wrapped it around his feet and lowered him head first down near the water. At this point, he was starting to shut up. As a group, we decided that we would not dunk him. We would take him down and just leave him tied up until Msgr. Dunn came visiting tomorrow. Mr. Ahern was smart enough to keep his mouth shut for the rest of the night. Nobody got any sleep. When we got up in the morning we all had breakfast. Someone fed Mr. Ahern but we did not untie him.

Sure enough, about noon, Monsignor Dunn came into our camp. When we saw him coming we let John go. He didn't know exactly what to do and we all waited until Msgr. Dunn came into the camp. This was one of the longest afternoons I have ever had. Monsignor Dunn talked to every single scout and to our scout leader. We were there at the campsite for two hours. When it was over, we all packed up our stuff and went home. It took a week before we heard what was going to happen. The result of it all was that John was not going to remain as the St. Columbkille scout leader and Tom and I were not going to be Boy Scouts.

The YMCA Swimming Pool Social Experiment

Mom and Dad's effort to help Tom and me meet people and to be more sociable was not off to a good start. Then they came up with a new idea. The YMCA downtown had a basketball gym and a swimming pool that was open to grade-school kids three days a week. They had it set up so that the guys didn't have to put up with the girls at the gym or the pool because they both had separate times in the pool. To Mom and Dad this seemed to be an opportunity that was worth a try. One Friday afternoon Mom took Tom and me down to the YMCA and they showed us around.

It was a really nice swimming pool. It was not nearly as big as the Dubuque City Pool at the north end of town where Tom and I had already learned to swim but the pool had two high-diving boards at one end of the pool. The gym was okay too.

After a couple visits to the pool, we decided we really liked it. The nicest part was the high dive. If you jumped in with your feet straight down after the highest possible board lift that you could get, you went straight into the water and touched the bottom of the pool. In a half a second you could propel yourself up out of the water three or four feet. That was fun! Neither Tom nor I knew much about diving. I tried to jump high and reach down and touch my toes before I hit the water. It took a while but I was starting to get the hang of it. The other guys were nice enough. We found out they went to some grade schools in Dubuque that I didn't even know about.

Then one day while we were in the pool, and Tom was doing some high diving, this big guy we had never seen before came into the pool and went up to the high dive. He walked out to the end of the diving board and he just stood there. He would take time rubbing his hands over his arm muscles and flexing his leg muscles so they were moving as he stood out on the diving board. This went on for a full five minutes as he took one different pose after another. The next thing I knew, Tom was climbing up the high-diving board ladder. I knew what this was going to be. Sure enough, Tom walked straight out to the end of the board and pushed him off. He fell on his face on top of the water and came up mad. He swam as fast as he could to the edge of the pool, jumped out and went for Tom. I got to Tom first.

He said some interesting cusswords. I don't remember specifically what they were but my memory tells me they were imaginative. We stood in front of one another for a minute and a couple of his buddies came up and stood beside him. I told him that we were new members of the YMCA and we didn't want to be in a fight in the pool and lose our membership. I thought that he didn't want that to happen either. He looked at me, didn't say anything for a minute and then said: "Okay." We agreed to meet in a half hour in the alley behind the swimming pool. Tom and I got dressed and knew that we had better do this right if we were going to survive. We decided not to use the defensive circle because they were a little too big to be knocked off balance with a surprise punch.

We got to the alley first. There was a two-step platform right below the door that they had to step down on in order to get to where we were on the cement in the alley. Big Muscle came out first. As he stepped down the two steps I took a step toward him and hit him in the jaw as hard as I could. He did not fall completely down but it gave Tom and me a shot at the other two guys. Both of them couldn't believe what happened. We were able to finish both of them off before Big Muscle regained his senses. That left both Tom and me with Big Muscle. It didn't take long before we could walk away knowing that none of them were going to follow us.

We got on the bus and went home. At dinner Mom asked us if we had a good time and we told her that we did. I looked at Tom and Tom looked at me. We decided to tell her everything that happened and we did. Dad didn't think it would be a good idea for us to go back to the pool. He figured that Big Muscle would be waiting for us and there would be no element of surprise. I think both Mom and Dad were disappointed that Tom and I had so little success in socializing and meeting new people that summer. We heard Dad tell Mom not to worry about it. Dad's theory was that we would grow up sooner or later and at least we were both alive and healthy. I always liked the way Dad thought.

Climbing Out of the Second-Story Window of Our New Garage

Dad always wanted a garage so that he did not have to park his car on York Street. He and Grandpa Schiltz got together and designed a garage that would be attached right to and become part of the back of the house with its door facing York Street. It was a neat design because it was not only a garage but a walkway from the basement where Mom's washing machine was. Mom could go through the garage in front of where the car was parked in the garage and out a west door to her clothesline poles. Aside from those convenience features the whole garage had a flat roof where we could eat dinner in the evenings under the shade of the tree. Mom could even walk west right out of her kitchen door and upstairs to the flat roof or downstairs to our north yard that we shared with the Dolphin family. Grandpa took the old Model-A garage apart and stored the material in his shed so that the backyard was much more open. Tom and I did whatever we could to help build the garage. We helped pour the cement for both the garage and the driveway. Mom and Dad really liked the garage and we used it as a place to eat dinner on its flat roof many times in the summer.

When we were in fourth or fifth grades, if we were not sleeping out in the backyard in the shack, we had to go to bed at ten o'clock. Neither one of us was ready to go to sleep at ten o'clock in the summer. Somehow sometime between 9:30 and 11:00 Tom and I would always end up wrestling on our bedroom floor. After a few minutes, our tussling would start the chandelier in the dining room right below our bedroom moving and tinkling. Sooner or later Dad would come up to our bedroom. We bent over the toy box. Dad would spank us and tell us to go to sleep. Finally we would. After our tussling went on for two or three nights Dad started to get mad at us. We could hear Mom at the bottom of the stairs saying: "Don't do it Joe." That didn't stop Dad. We got used to our evening spankings. I remember once when Dad came in to our bedroom and motioned for Tom to bend over the toy box. Tom pleaded: "I want to told you something." That delayed the inevitable for fifteen seconds. I still smile when I remember it.

Looking back at it, the new garage was one of the better things that ever happened to Tom and me. It did not take us long to figure out all we had to do to get out of our bedroom was open the window on York Street, step out of the second-floor window onto the shingled first-floor window shade, and then right onto the garage's flat roof. There was even a wooden railing system around the edge of the garage that made it possible for us to grab for balance. Getting down to the yard was no big deal. All we had to do was hang on to the edge of the flat roof and drop three or so feet to the yard. Getting back into the bedroom was easy. We would jump up and grab ahold of the edge of the flat roof, swing onto the top, and then step into the first-floor window.

During the summer that I was in sixth grade, the new garage added a lot of fun to Tom and my family's lives. All we had to do was open the York Street window, climb down to the yard and explore the world. We could go into the shack or we could get an apple or some cherries or just sit on the front porch and watch cars go by. That really worked. After a while, we both got tired and climbed back up into our bedroom and finally went to sleep. It was nice to know that we could get an apple at night if we really needed one without disturbing Mom or Dad.

Grandpa Schiltz's Wallpaper-Steaming Jobs

Grandpa Schiltz owned all six apartment houses on the east side of Nevada Street across from the Nativity Church. Grandpa and Grandma Schiltz lived in their own apartment house on the second floor of 125 Nevada Street. Whenever someone would move from one of the apartment houses Grandpa would ask Tom and me to steam off the wallpaper in the apartment. This was a messy, dirty, stinky, hot job.

Tom and I would walk over to Grandpa Schiltz's house early in the morning and meet Grandpa at the back of his house where he had all of his tools in his two garages. Grandpa would get out his two steamers and fill them up with water. He would open the door to the vacant apartment and tell us to work together in the same room. We'd have to finish one room at a time so that he could come back and do the final clean up before new wallpaper was to be put on the walls. Grandpa would show us where the bathroom was and tell us he would be back with some lunch about noon.

It did not take a lot of smarts to run the steamer. First, you loosened the wallpaper up with the steam and then you scraped the wallpaper from the wall with a wide putty knife. Some of the wallpaper fell onto the canvas on the floor. Some of it did not leave the wall until you scraped it or steamed it again. There was no way that hot wallpaper did not get onto your hands. It was a messy, messy job. Tom and I tried to stay out of the way of one another but it did not always work. Sooner or later some of my hot scrapings hit Tom and Tom's would hit me. This went on all morning until the inevitable happened. Tom and I would wrestle. We knew better than to fight one another but that did not stop us from wrestling in the mess on the floor. It was always about this time that Grandpa Schiltz came into the room with our lunch and something cold to drink. Grandpa would tell us we were doing a good job. Then he would eat lunch and visit with us.

It almost never took us any longer than the afternoon to finish the job. At about three o'clock, Grandpa would come over to where we were working to help us clean up the room. We'd take the dirty tarpaulin into the backyard and sweep it off so it was ready for the next job. The three of us were good team. Tom and I had a job like this maybe once a month or maybe not quite so often. I remember one time when we worked into the evening and Grandma Schiltz cooked a wonderful meal for us all. Grandpa Schiltz was a lucky man. Grandma really loved Grandpa and she was a wonderful cook. For years every time we went to Grandpa's house he always took us to his garages and showed us all of his tools. These were the times when Tom and I learned how to really use Grandpa's carpentry tools. Boy did that payoff throughout our lives!

Pouring Andy Kisting's Cement Driveway for Grandpa Schiltz

In our summertime travels with Grandpa Schiltz and in helping Dad and Grandpa Schiltz build our garage at 135 South Hill Street Tom and I learned a lot about pouring cement driveways and sidewalks, how to use the tools, etc. One summer Dad had promised a friend of his, Andy Kisting, that he would work with Grandpa Schiltz to find some time to tear out and replace his old cement driveway to his garage. Mr. Kisting lived about halfway between our house on South Hill Street and Grandpa Schlitz's house on Nevada Street. Because Grandpa's youngest son, our uncle Jack Schiltz, was busy building houses. Grandpa asked Tom and me if we would do the job. Of course we said yes.

We walked across Dodge Street to the Kisting house and met Grandpa with his truck. Grandpa had all the two-by-four boards, stakes, sledgehammers, shovels, nails, saws, and everything we needed. It took Tom and I almost a day to break up the old cement even though it was not in good shape. It took three loads to haul away all the broken cement in Grandpa's truck. I don't remember where we dumped the cement. It was a lot easier to unload than it was to load it in the first place. Once we got rid of the old cement, we framed up what would be the new driveway. We were not exactly sure how to tie in the sidewalk to the house to the street entrance to the garage. We measured it out and staked all of the two-by-fours where we thought they should be. It took us almost all morning to get that much done.

When Grandpa came he had some suggestions on how we could improve what we had done. Tom looked at me, and I looked at him, and we told Grandpa we would do it. That was when Tom had an idea: "Why don't we bring little brother Joe over here while we redo this framework?" It was really, really hot that day. We noticed that the neighbor ladies were all watching what we were doing. We figured that if we got our brother, little Joe, out here sweating with us, the neighbor ladies would bring us cold drinks and maybe even some ice cream. We should not have had to do that except for the fact that the Kistings were on vacation. We were there on the job alone.

When we went back home and had lunch We offered our brother Joe an opportunity to make some money with us. He agreed. Boy, did that pay off! We were reworking the two-by-four frame for an hour when one of the neighbor ladies came out with ice-cold drinks. Every hour after that someone came up and offered us something cold to drink. At about 4 o'clock, Grandpa came by and approved everything we did. He left the long bull float we had to use to finish the surface of the cement. It was a clumsy tool with its ten-foot-long handle. There was no substitute for it as it was the only way you could get the wide cement uniformly smooth.

At the end of the day we were ready to pour the cement. Grandpa told us that the cement truck would be there tomorrow morning at eight o'clock but he may or may not be able to be there that early. That did not bother Tom and me. We had done this cement finish work two times before when we worked with Grandpa's youngest son, Uncle Jack. The hard part was not finishing the cement. It was putting in the dividers so that the driveway stayed together as a unit. If we divided the cement correctly, each piece would always remain square and clean. Dividing the cement required a long thin strip of plywood. Tom or I would walk on top of the cement on the plywood and use the plywood to run the divider in a straight line. It was no big deal to smooth out the cement where the plywood was laying.

We had no sooner gotten to the Kistings in the morning when a city inspector showed up. The inspector got out of his truck, came over to Tom, Joe, and I and asked: "You got a building permit?" I told him we didn't know anything about a permit and didn't know what he was talking about. He then explained what the rules were and why we needed a permit. We didn't say anything. We just let him talk. Finally, he asked: "You working for someone?" I told him we were not working for anyone; we were doing this for our grandfather.

"So who is your grandfather?" he asked. I told him it was Harry Schiltz. When he heard me say Grandpa Schiltz's name a smile came to his face. I asked him if he knew Grandpa. He told me that everyone in the city knew Grandpa Schiltz. He said Grandpa was one of a handful of people who set up Iowa's first savings and loan banks so that people could save money and build their own houses. I did not know that! I told the inspector that Grandpa would be here shortly as would the cement truck. He said it was okay. He knew that if this was Grandpa's job that he had the permit. He told us to do a good job for Grandpa.

The driveway and sidewalk turned out fine. It took most of the day to finish, remove the frame forms and fill the frame holes with dirt. Our family has always known how to work together.

Our Mom and Dad always stayed friends with the Kistings. In fact, they are still together. Our Mom and Dad and the Kistings are both buried side-by-side in mausoleums at Mount Calvary Cemetery in Dubuque.

Grade School Football at Saint Columbkille' s

Seventh-grade football was a real challenge. The eighth graders had almost full control over the team. While both seventh and eighth grade guys worked out on the field together we knew the only people who were going to routinely play were the eighth graders. We all traveled together when we played at someone else's field but only a few of us seventh graders got a chance to play. Those few included John Cady who played fullback and John Conley who sometimes played quarterback. The rest of us seventh graders had to concentrate on developing football blocking and tackling skills. St. Columbkille had a fifty-fifty year when I was in seventh grade. I played a little bit and we won as many as we lost.

I had to practice first at school and then second at home with Dad. I would tell Dad what happened to me, how I got blindsided from the side and how I was always two steps late from being in a position to either block or tackle. Dad showed me how to use both of my arms, how to run sideways while directly watching the play, and thank God, how to tackle and block. I found out that it was more than just timing and getting an angle on someone so that you did not hit the player straight on. The key was to figure out what the play was in the first second or two so that I could be in the right place at the right time. Knowing *how* to do this was the key to being able to play and keeping this a fun and challenging game.

Our coach was Father Duane Raftis. Father Raftis spent almost all of his time teaching basic blocking schemes, how to tackle, and who does what in running the plays. What he taught us worked most of the time but many things just did not seem to happen as planned. Even so, everyone always did their very best in the game. After we had played a couple games, Father Raftis decided that John Conley, a seventh grader in our class, was to be our quarterback. That worked out pretty good because John could throw the football with some accuracy. John Cady also became a halfback. John did pretty well despite not getting much blocking. Seventh grade was a good learning year. It was apparent to me that our class had enough athletes that maybe we could win the Dubuque championship next year when we were in eighth grade.

When our eighth grade year came around everybody in the class was looking forward to it. We only had about three weeks of practice before we played our first game. After one week it became apparent to me that our class was divided in itself. John Conley was our quarterback and I played backup quarterback and left end. Conley always favored using his buddies when calling plays. Because of this the team was emotionally divided between his few buddies and the rest of us. I talked to Dad about it and he said that this was something that the team itself had to fix. He did not know if Father Raftis could do it on his own.

Dad asked me if I thought I could take John Conley. I told him I thought I could but it would be close. John was bigger and stronger, but I was faster and had some experience dealing with this kind of a problem. John was not stupid. He would know what was on my mind if I tried to force him to listen to me. Then I got an idea. I asked Dad what he thought of me asking Father Raftis to referee at some private location where no one else was around. We both figured that Father knew what the problem was and thought that he might go along with it.

The next day after school, and before football practice, I talked to Father Raftis and told him what I wanted to do and why I wanted him to be there. With Father there, it would be impossible for John not to believe that it was necessary for him to be a better leader if our team was going to succeed. Father listened and told me he would get back to me. A half an hour later he said he would help and that he would ask John and I both to meet him on the east side of the football field below what was then a rock wall where no one could see us.

John knew that something was up. We had a better practice than normal. After practice when everyone was gone the three of us went down by the rock wall. I tried to explain to John that he was the problem and unless he changed, our team would never win the city championship. I watched him real close as I was talking and explained to him how he was being a total asshole. As the conversation went on, I watched him more carefully. He feigned indifference and then took a shot at me with his right hand. I saw it coming, blocked it with my left hand and hit him three times in the face before he fell to the ground. I sat on him and yelled at him that he needed to change if our team was ever going to have a chance. When I finally shut up, he had a funny expression on his face. I looked around and Father Raftis was gone. I let John up and we talked for a while. We both agreed that we were going to do our best to win the city championship. I can't remember for sure, but I think we shook hands on it.

You would not believe how our team came together after that. John Cady became a full-time fullback and I played left end where I could catch and block and, more importantly, tackle. As Dad taught me, my secret was to be in the right place at the WRONG time for the other team.

St. Columbkille won its first three games. The last championship game was against Nativity Church and it was going to be played at Saint Columbkille. Everybody came to all of the games. That included Mom, Dad, Tom, Joe, John and everybody in all of our classes. The whole crowd was repeated for the Nativity team. The stands were full and kids were all around the football field.

Two days before the game I had twisted my left ankle a little bit and had to keep it tightly wrapped in order to be able to run well. While running didn't seem to be a problem, I could not move quickly side to side. Because of this, another classmate played my left end position. I played left linebacker on defense. The game went just as predicted. John Cady had a few great yards playing fullback. John

Conley had at least three successful passes. At the end of the first half the score was 7 to 7 and no one knew how the game was going to turn out.

With the beginning of the second half, I was able to throw a key block for John Cady and he gained ten yards and a touchdown to put us one touchdown ahead. As we got to the halfway point of the fourth quarter, Nativity started to have some running success with their fullback, Jim Krippus. I finally figured out what they were doing. Their line would take a two-step fake one way and then block the other way. Krippus would do the same. This always seemed to leave a hole in our line between the guard and tackle. We would always catch him but not before he made five yards.

I changed places with our guy in the defensive backfield just behind Nativity's center. Time was running out and it was now or never to stop them. Nativity called their next play. Their line took two steps to the left then turned right. There was a big hole between their center and guard position. I knew that Jim Krippus was going to be coming through that hole but I did not have the time or space to get an angle on the hole. I had to hit it straight on. I guessed right and tackled Krippus while he was still in the hole. Making that tackle head on was the only thing I remembered. Two days later I asked Mom how the game turned out. She told me that St. Columbkille had won the game and that I and the rest of the team had a big ice cream celebration after our victory. I did not remember a single thing about either the celebration or two days after the celebration.

CHAPTER 3—LONG LIVE LORAS ACADEMY

Loras Academy, Our Mixing Place

My father, Joseph Gill Graham, graduated from Columbia Academy in 1931. When I graduated from eighth grade at Saint Columbkille, Columbia Academy had become Loras Academy. Both Columbia and Loras high schools were in the same buildings. They both had students not only from Dubuque but also from surrounding Iowa cities as well as from Illinois and Wisconsin cities and towns. My memory tells me that almost half of the students lived at the academy in dormitory rooms. Dad's yearbook, PURGOLD 1931, shows that most of the teachers were priests. What the yearbook does not say is that many of the priests lived at the academy. As a matter of fact, Mom and Dad told me that they named me, their first son, after the Rev. Emmett Kelly, but that's another story for another day.

Being an all-boys school, Loras Academy was a wonderful place to meet guys from everywhere. They not only came from all of the other parishes in Dubuque but they came from places I knew nothing about. In the classroom they all talked the same. At noon we all took a break and ate lunch at the academy cafeteria located just behind the big school building. The cafeteria was a neat place. You had to enter the cafeteria down a long narrow corridor, and at the end it opened up into a big dining place with tables and chairs and a long serving line. It did not take long for lunch. Everybody grabbed the same thing, ate it in five minutes at the table and left to do something outside. Every square inch of the school building was used. The third floor had a huge open study hall. Many of the dorm and priest rooms were on the third floor as well.

The high-school girl situation was not that simple. There were three girl high schools. The one I was most familiar with was the Visitation Academy. This is where my two aunts, Sister Patricia and Sister Irene Graham taught. The other two girl schools were the Immaculate Conception on Davis Street near Stone Hill and St. Joseph's Academy on South Algona Street. As interesting as the classes were, one of our first concerns was how to meet girls. To begin with, I was not all that sure why anybody would want to do that.

Meeting girls was pretty hard to avoid when you consider that every Friday night there was a mixer at the Loras Academy gym where everybody came to dance. I had never been very good at remembering people's names. I used a small spiral notebook where I wrote down the names, addresses and telephone numbers of the girls I danced with. As my freshman year proceeded it was a good thing I had my notebook. The girls seemed to be impressed if you remembered their names. I was impressed by the fact that some of these girls really knew how to dance. This was where I learned how to dance the jitterbug. At the end of the year I started to get good at it.

It's Not Easy Being a Freshman

There was one event when I was a freshman at Loras Academy that I wasn't all that proud of, and yet looking back at it I think it changed the way I thought about what was funny and what was not. I think my first English class instructor was Father Paul Grace. I remember that there was one of my classmates that I thought deserved to be smashed on the side of his head by a strong rubber-band-slung slightly wet spit wad. I would not have thought so if he did not truly deserve it. To make a long story short this was an activity that I almost never missed. However, in order to assure success, it takes one full second in order to obtain a perfect aim. While I was in the process of assuring my success, Father Grace turned around and caught me red-handed in my momentary aiming pause. I had to apologize in front of the whole class and Father Grace made me correct the class papers for the whole week for him as a penalty. That was not a problem because I got what I deserved. What came next was a problem.

Father Grace drove a small VW car to school. from wherever he lived when he came to the Academy to teach. He always parked his car on Loras Boulevard next to the academy building. The building had two stone columns that stuck out from the building's wall almost three feet. Some of the guys noticed that Father Grace's car would physically fit between these two stone columns and thought it would be funny if we could put his car in there where he could not drive out because there wasn't enough room to maneuver the car.

The more we thought about it the funnier it got. I came up with an idea. We got three guys on the front and three guys on the back and started bouncing the car up from front to back until we were able to bounce the right side tires up over the curb. Soon thereafter the left side tires were also on the sidewalk next to the building. It did not take much bouncing after that to put the car in between the two columns without a scrape or a dent or anything happening to the car.

We all hung out in front of the school before we went home just like we always did and we were there talking to one another when Father Grace came out and saw his car. He stood there staring at the car for maybe two full minutes without saying a word. This was a world that Father Grace knew nothing about. I could imagine him thinking, *How did my car get in there?* I realized that he did not have a lot of faculty friends who could help him out. While this was funny to us, he had no solution. At that moment I knew that we should not have done this. I stepped up to Father and told him a lie. I told him that I didn't know how all of this happened. I asked all the guys to help me remove his car. Everybody stepped in and we tried to pull the car out but that did not work. We knew it would not. Then we started to bounce the car and finally returned the car to the street. Father Grace thanked us. I never pulled anything like that again on

Father Grace or any other teacher at Loras Academy. That was one of the better decisions I ever made. Between the end of my freshman year and beginning of my sophomore year, I was able to thank God for having done so.

I remember one day I was on the third floor of the academy just after the last study hall had been let out and everybody was on their way home. There were two guys halfway down the hall near the door to the restroom and the water fountain. The one guy was yelling and swearing at the other. All this time Father Sims was walking down the hall toward the restroom reading his Breviary prayer book. Without his eyes leaving his reading, Father Sims just walked down the hall until he got to the two students. At that point he folded his Breviary under his arm, grabbed the kid who was cussing and smacked him with his right hand. The kid slumped down and sat on the floor with his back to the wall and a blank stare on his face. Father Sims reopened his Breviary and continued slowly walking down the hall.

Now I understood what had happened in the big study hall the day before. When I walked into the study hall that day every one of the sixty desks in the study hall was filled with somebody reading or working on coursework. No one was messing around. No one was talking. No one was throwing anything. I could not believe what I was seeing. There were at least six of the academy's biggest goof-offs in this one room and no one was doing anything. This did not make any sense. There was not even anyone sitting in the room monitor's desk. I sat down and started to do my homework when Father Sims walked into the room and sat at his desk. I asked myself: *Where have I seen this before?* Then I remembered, Sister Mary Agatha.

I got to know Father Sims a lot better in my sophomore year at Loras Academy. In my freshman year I played football with Bob Keyes, my cousin, and had a lot of fun. As a freshman I was still able to handle myself in dealing with the bigger kids. Freshman did not get to play in the games much. Practice was a challenge but still fun. When we started playing football in my sophomore year I began to notice that everybody had gained at least fifteen pounds and two inches, except me. I was still able to handle myself and was now beginning to have an opportunity to play as part of the team. I began asking myself what would happen to me if I got blindsided by one of those big guys. I thought about that for a couple weeks and then I went to talk to Father Sims. I told him there were a lot of other things I wanted to do at the academy, that I didn't think it was all that smart to try to play football for three more years. He pointed out that I could still take care of myself and would play some. We both thought it might be a good idea for me to do other things. I thanked him and turned my attention to other things.

Saving Brother Tom—Father Roger O'Brien

In my sophomore year, my brother Tom was a freshman at Loras Academy. While we walked to school together we didn't really see much of one another during the day. One of the few times we could be together was at lunchtime. This was when we would both go to the academy's cafeteria to eat. I remember one day I was coming out of school into the parking lot between the school building and the cafeteria. I saw Tom was in trouble! Tom had one guy holding his right arm and the second guy holding his left arm. A third guy stood in front of him yelling at him.

I ran to the scene and poked the third guy on the shoulder. As he turned around I hit him in the face as hard as I could. He dropped. Tom shook his right hand loose and I went for that guy while Tom went to the guy who was still holding his left hand. It took a lot more than just one punch to drop the other two, but they went down. At this point several guys started moving toward Tom and me.

We started to back into the narrow corridor of the cafeteria where they could only come at us one at a time. Between the two of us we dropped two more before it was over. Then we got lunch.

The next thing I knew there was someone knocking on my class door. Our instructor went to the door to find out what it was all about. To make a long story short, I ended up in the office of the academy's principal, Father Roger O'Brien. He had a nice people-friendly office with a big desk and a big window where he could look out and see the traffic on Loras Boulevard. There were all kinds of certificates, pictures and trophies on shelves and a big rug on the floor. There was a chair in the middle of the room in front of his desk. He told me in a very firm voice to sit down. Father O'Brien asked me to explain what happened at lunch that day. I told him the same story I told you but it did not change his expression. He told me this was a wonderful school and he was not going to put up with that kind of fighting. It was my responsibility to figure out how to get along with everybody. I told him all I was doing was protecting my brother but he did not accept that a reasonable excuse.

He rose to his feet from behind the desk and pointed his finger right at me. He told me he wanted me to promise this would never happen again. I told him I could not and would NEVER make that promise. I told him I had already promised my father, Joseph Graham that I would do whatever was necessary to protect my younger brother and that I meant to keep that promise. I told Father O'Brien he should call my father and get his permission for me to make the promise he was asking me to make to him. Father O'Brien looked at me funny, scolded me again, and told me he would call my dad. I am sure that Dad would have told me if he received a call from Father O'Brien. The subject never came up again. Tom and I never had any trouble like that again.

The Drill Team—Captain Howard Boston, the Decider

Sometime in the beginning of my sophomore year after I decided to leave the football team, there was an announcement that Capt. Boston was considering the establishment of a ROTC drill team. The academy had not had a drill team for a couple of years. I thought that this would be fun. This was an opportunity for my brother Tom and my friends John Ryan, Peter Elmer and me to put a drill team together. The juniors and seniors were busy with other things. We had to concentrate our recruiting in the sophomore and freshman classes. It took us a couple of weeks to put forty cadets together.

I remember where we all first met with our Commanding Officer Capt. Boston. There we were standing together in front of his office when I told him we were willing to work and create a drill team. Capt. Boston looked at us funny and told us he had not had an opportunity to do any recruiting. We told him he did not have to recruit, that we would be the team. There was a long silence as he looked at us. He finally said: "That's fine" and told us to meet him on the football practice field tomorrow after school.

The drill team was a lot of fun, but getting forty people in total sync with one another was also hard work. By the time we were juniors and seniors we had an outstanding drill team. The Academy had us marching and drilling in city parades on holidays, at halftime football games and every other excuse or location we could come up with. This was one of the few places where Tom, my St. Columbkille classmate Peter Elmer, John Ryan, and I could work together. I was always the drill team commander and Tom was always one of the drill team squad leaders. We really enjoyed doing it. I had no way of knowing how all of this military etiquette would pay off later after I graduated from Loras Academy, but that's another story.

The Rifle Team and My Dream to Be a Pilot

I always thought that being on the academy's rifle team would be a natural for me. Being a military academy it had a long history of rifle teams but the teams always had mixed success. They won some and lost some. The rifle team basically broke even with the six or eight rifle teams that they were routinely competing with and also on a national basis. Given the fact that I had multiple years of experience and success with BB guns, I figured this would be fun. I was not wrong. Before the year was over Loras Academy had won every single one of its fifteen postal matches. The rifle team also finished thirteenth out of ninety-five teams competing in the Fifth Army ROTC rifle team contest. I was right about my ability to shoot. Even so, it was hard for me to make the top five scorers in each match so that my score would be part of the winning score. I learned how to relax, how to hold the rifle firmly and gently at the same time, and how to breathe softly while slowly pulling the trigger.

I knew that Jim Trosky and Bob Schlegel were as good a shot as I was but not better. I could not figure out why their scores were always a few points better than mine. After two or three rifle team matches, Mom suggested that I go and see an eye doctor. I explained to her that I always wanted to be a pilot and that it was my understanding that pilots had to have perfect vision. Mom's response was that God gave me the tools I have and that I was responsible to make the best use of them. She told me this may be a way that I find out whether or not I was really meant to be a pilot. If I needed glasses and I still wanted to compete at the highest possible level in the rifle team, I may have to get glasses. I could not defeat Mom's logic and decided that I would have my eyes checked.

Mom was right. Glasses made a huge difference. I could see each bull's-eye and every mark on the target crystal-clear. I don't know whether this was all real or all mental. It really doesn't matter because after I got glasses I always shot in the top three. Once in a while I shot as number one. The rifle team was truly a team just as the drill team was. Working together and helping one another gave every member of both teams a sense of real pride in accomplishment.

Loras Academy's ROTC program was a wonderful thing. It provided many chances for the whole class to work together as a team in the same way that athletic programs did. In some ways, ROTC was even better because the direction for what was going on or what they wanted to do came almost exclusively from the cadets themselves. For me it was natural. This was where I and many of my classmates discovered it was fun to try to be the best that we can be at what we do. In the end, it was my Company A that was selected best platoon in school. I got to hold the academy's annual best platoon traveling trophy, and get my picture taken, as company commander at the Academy's ROTC senior year awards ceremony.

MY WONDERFUL SOPHMORE SUMMER

Grandpa Schiltz's Slow Roof Job

I think this was where Grandpa Schiltz's youngest son, my uncle Jack, really grew up and became what he was meant to be. Grandpa assigned Tom and me to work with Jack to shingle a huge house. I cannot remember all about the house but it was a huge, beautiful, three-story house. It could have been a hundred-year-old house because it had a big two-story detached garage that could have been a stable for horses. It was Tom's and my job to carry the shingle bundles up a huge ladder and to distribute them on the roof. The roof itself was steep but it could still be walked on safely. Part of the problem was the length of the ladder. When Grandpa carried the ladder on his pickup truck rack it stuck out three feet in front and three feet in back of the pickup. When Tom and I did this job at other places we could theoretically, but maybe not safely, carry two bundles up the ladder and as long as we were slow and careful. You could not do that at this house. The ladder was much too long, and two bundles were too heavy.

Uncle Jack had two guys with him to do shingling. I remember one of the guy's names was Bones Kaufmann. I can't remember what the other guy's name was. Tom and I worked all morning carrying shingles one bundle at a time up the ladder onto the roof. We were both smart enough to take a break and rest once in a while. But we still continued carrying shingles all morning. Jack, Bones and the other guy spent most of the morning under a shade tree drinking beer telling stories and laughing. At about eleven o'clock they ran out of beer, went up on the roof and began shingling. It was about twelve o'clock when Grandpa showed up to see how everything was going. Grandpa climbed up the ladder and saw that Jack and his buddies had just gotten started shingling.

I'm not sure what story Jack told Grandpa, but Grandpa was not buying it. Grandpa Schiltz did not yell. He just looked at us and made us feel bad if we did not do something right. In this case Grandpa was mad. I could tell he was really not happy as he looked RIGHT at Uncle Jack as he was talking to him. Tom and I knew that Grandpa loved us and we were not about to lie to him. After Jack told his story to Grandpa, Grandpa turned to us and asked us what happened. After we told Grandpa what happened, Bones and the other guy left and never came back. Grandpa left our lunch with us and left in the pickup with Jack. We had a good lunch. Grandpa had included a cold Coca-Cola for us. When Grandpa brought Jack back he was alone. He told us that we should give Jack whatever help we could because Jack was going to be finishing the shingle job by himself and it was going to take a day or two longer.

I think the next two days were the easiest days at work that Tom and I ever had. We could not do any shingling to help Jack. All we did was clean up the cardboard wrappers and the straps that held the bundles together as they hit the ground when Jack was finished with them. After that, Jack was never the same. Jack still had his sense of humor but it seemed like he was happier. We never knew what they talked about. What was said was a breakthrough event for Uncle Jack. Soon after Jack became Grandpa's supervisor and probably a partial owner of Grandpa's whole business.

The Dyersville Church Picnic—Tom the Provider

This was a good summer. Tom and I got our first car. It was Grandpa Graham's old 1950 Nash Ambassador. It was a pukey light-green four-door car. The color reminded me of the first color of the sheets that Mom had dyed for Tom and me so we could steal some of the Blades' apples. While it was not the neatest car, it made it possible for us to go places and do things that otherwise we would have no opportunity to do. One of the first things that caught our eye was a spring picnic that was advertised in the *Telegraph Herald* for the coming Saturday at Dyersville the very next day. Jim Sievers, Tom, and I decided we would go to the picnic. Dyersville is only a few miles west of Dubuque on Highway 20. The church was easy to find. All we had to do was head for the tall church steeples that towered over the tree line of the town.

It was a beautiful day when we got there Saturday. I drove the car and parked it really close to all the gaming tables where everybody was trying not to lose too much money. We discovered that we only had seven dollars between the three of us. To make matters worse, I looked at the gas tank when we got out of the car and noticed it was nearly empty. I knew this was not a problem. I gave all my money to Tom so that he could gamble with it. I asked Jim Sievers to do the same but he was very hesitant. I told Jim that Tom was the luckiest man alive and that the only way we were going to get home was to have Tom win the money we needed. He finally agreed mainly because we didn't have any choice. As far as we knew, there were only three kids from Dyersville that went to Loras Academy. We really did not know any of them.

Tom did not let us down. Before the day was over we all ate three times, had plenty of pop, and filled up the gas tank. It really ended up being a glorious day. We even met some interesting and nice girls. It never hurts to have a little luck in the family.

Dump Truck and Other Dating

Grandpa Schiltz built our house at 135 South Hill Street a long time ago. The whole house was trimmed in beautiful solid oak. The winding stairs going up to the bedrooms were wonderful except for one thing. The original stain that Grandpa used had all turned dark and was almost black. Mom asked Tom and me if we would remove all of the original stain so that the original beautiful oak could be seen. Of course we agreed to do so. Mom had some really good stain remover and we went to work on it. It took us a couple of weeks before we got it all off so that the beauty of the original wood was now visible, not only on the stairs but also on all the windows, doors, dining room sliding door, and baseboards throughout the whole house. It was beautiful when it was finished. Mom was thinking ahead as we later found out.

It was about this time that Uncle Jack was playing poker with some of his buddies and had won a 1928 black dump truck. It was probably the ugliest truck I had ever seen. It had only a seat for the driver. The passenger seat was gone. The truck had not been cleaned for years. I wondered how they could keep the engine running so I opened the hood. Much to my surprise there was a two-gallon oil container that drained into the engine somehow when it was running. While the truck ran, it poured out an endless stream of smoke that got bigger the faster you ran the engine. I noticed that if you really gunned the engine, it created a cloud of smoke bigger than the truck itself.

I asked Uncle Jack if I cleaned up the truck for him could I use it for dating. He looked at me funny smiled and said yes, provided I had the truck back Monday morning full of gas and oil. It took four hours of high pressure hose cleaning, scraping and repairing before I could even think about inviting girls to ride in the back of the truck or sit next to me in its cab. The cab passenger seat was a brand-new peach crate covered with a clean blanket. While the passenger seat rider had to hang on to the door handle to sit upright, the seat itself was very comfortable.

Uncle Jack's 1928 truck really helped me figure out which girls had a sufficient sense of humor, were fun to be with, and worth dating. Tom and I met two fun-loving girls who were willing to play with us and our truck. At our early Loras dances we met Kathleen Zwack, who lived on Alta Vista Street across from the Visitation Academy and Cathy Meyer, who lived right next to Eagle Point Park on the top of the hill overlooking the Mississippi River dam. I remember a time when Kathy Meyer and Kathleen Zwack called four of their girlfriends, we called four other guys, and we were all to meet at the tennis courts in Eagle Point Park to play volleyball.

I picked up Kathleen Zwack. Kathleen sat on the cab passenger peach-crate seat. Kathleen and I then picked up four more girls and they rode in the back of the truck. Tom picked up the guys. They were to meet us at the park. When Kathleen and I got to the long, steep road leading up to the park, it was apparent to all of us that the dump truck was not strong enough to take us all the way up the hill to the park. So the girls in the back got out and helped push the dump truck up to the park. As we were moving slowly along, Tom came by in our Nash. They drove around us laughing all the way. We all had a good time. We reminded one another of that nonsense for a long time thereafter.

Jack's dump truck came in real handy one other time. The way it started was my aunt, Sister Mary Patricia told me about this nice girl. I will call her Alice as I cannot remember her name. She was in Sister Patricia's class at the Visitation Academy. I agreed to meet her. We went out for some ice cream and then down to Frentress Lake to the Graham family cottage on the Illinois side of the Mississippi River. We walked up and down the beaches just talking. She seemed nice at the time. I finally decided that Sister Patricia was right and invited her to go with me to the Loras Academy–sponsored dance that was going to be held on the north end of town next to the river in the Melody Mill ballroom. She thanked me and told me she would be happy to go. Since the dance was three weeks away she had plenty of time to get ready. Then came an unanticipated turn of events.

After I had agreed to take Alice to the dance, she called and told me what I should wear. She asked me if I would put it on so she could see it when I picked her up after school to go get some ice cream. I had not made up my mind what I was going to wear but I put on something and went to pick her up. When we got to the ice cream place she told me that what I had on clashed with what she had intended to wear. There were several things I could have worn that would not have clashed with her dress. She explained two or three of them to me. The next thing that had to be straightened out was the color of the flowers I was to give to her.

After an hour or so we got this all straightened out and I took her home. She lived in a fancy house that had a semicircular driveway.

You could drive in at one entrance from the street circle in front of her front door and the drive out the second entrance to the street. The front yard had a lot of nice trees and shrubs. I dropped her off in the Nash in front of her front door. We walked in and I met her mother. Alice told her mother everything we had decided. They both seem pleased. I told them that I really did not need the pop they offered and went home.

This was not good! Alice and I had nothing in common. I was not even sure if she had a sense of humor. I remembered my promise to Mom, that I would treat girls with respect and keep any promise I made to them. After thinking about it, I came up with a plan and asked Uncle Jack if I could use is 1928 dump truck to go on a date on the weekend. He told me I could. That afternoon I took the truck and cleaned it as thoroughly as I could. I replaced the peach crate passenger seat and put on a clean blanket for her to sit on. Just as she had asked I wore what she wanted me to and I had the right flowers. When I went to pick her up I drove in the semicircular driveway first entrance and parked right in front of their front door. Before I turned the truck off I revved it up. The smoke covered the front door and was high enough to go into the windows on the second floor. It's a good thing that the windows were not open, but the front door was.

As I walked into the house with the flowers in hand, Alice and her mother were huddled together sometimes screaming, sometimes talking. Her father was on the stairway up to the second floor. He saw everything but he could not laugh. He knew his life would be over if he laughed. I just stopped there in the doorway for a couple of minutes while they made up their minds if she would go to the dance. As we drove out of her driveway, she asked me if I would be kind enough to use the backroads to get to the dance. I told her that I would and we did. Alice asked me to drop her off in the parking lot. I told her it was not polite and pulled right up to the main entrance and stopped. When I got there I revved up the truck so she could walk through the smoke to the dance floor.

After I got the truck parked and entered the dance floor I noticed on the other side of the dance floor that Alice was talking to a whole group of girls. She would talk and then point at me from across the dance floor. Then she would talk some more and point me again. It was apparent that all of the girls felt sorry for her. When I told my buddies what happened I thought two of them would die laughing. But I was wrong. They all survived. Apparently Alice got a ride home from someone else. All I knew was that no one else ever tried to get a date for me again.

Dancing at 135 South Hill Street

The original furnace at 135 South Hill was coal. Tom and I would get up in the morning and fill the coal bin so the house would stay warm all day. It wasn't long after Tom and I started at Loras Academy when Dad changed the furnace to gas. This made it possible to turn the basement into a place to play or visit. We cleaned it up and washed and painted the walls and floor. You would never know there was ever any coal in the basement. The new furnace was no longer in the middle of the room. Dad decided he would put in a bathroom toilet stool and sink so people could wash up. We knew how to clean the walls. The problem was how to divide off the furnace from the rest of the basement and the laundry room. The bigger problem was what to use to make the divider. We did not want plywood so we looked for a way to give the basement a finished house look.

We both looked through Grandpa Schiltz's shed for building materials. We could not believe what we found. There was a huge stack of beautifully stained, beech wood boards we could use for paneling. We looked at one another and knew we had found the answer. We told Dad how we planned to divide up the basement using the beech wood as panels. Dad showed us how to divide off the bathroom and Grandpa told us we could have the beech wood. In a month the basement was a fun place to be. The ceiling was not hard to cover and Grandpa had the ceiling tile to do it. I don't think we had to add any electrical outlets as Grandpa's original design of the house had put in everything that was needed.

We asked Mom and Dad if we could invite girls to dance with us in the basement. They encouraged us to do it. At this point I had gotten to know and like Kathleen Zwack, and Tom was still dating Kathy Meyer. We invited some of our Loras Academy classmates to join us dancing in the basement as we often did all winter long. The classmate that I remember the most at this time in high school was George Chapman. It was many years later that I found out that George had married the girl he dated and danced with in our basement.

STRETCHING OUR WINGS AT THE ACADEMY

Student Council Innovation and Tragedy

My junior year, and Tom's sophomore year, at the academy were both magic and enlightening. Everything was going well with the drill team and the rifle team. I continued to have some fun serving on the student council. The junior year student council service tended to confirm my prior observation that the student council could do a lot more than what it was doing to promote and encourage additional contacts with both the Loras Academy faculty and the other three girl schools. I thought that faculty reports on school management issues would be informative and probably fun if we found out what made things tick at the school. It also made me smile when I thought about being on an interschool student committee with the girl schools and considering how to better plan interschool activities.

The more I thought about it the clearer it became. It would be fun just to raise these issues. In the end I decided to run for Student Council President. As soon as I made that decision, several guys from my class and Tom's class offered to help. Among the several people who offered to help us do things, it was Ken Dempsey who helped Tom and me do the campaign planning. We even had a member of the freshman class on our committee. His name was Richard "Dick" Kehoe. The four of us got together a couple of times a week to share ideas, compare notes and to try to figure out the best way to contact people. What the student council did was not the first thing on anyone's mind. Even so, at least everyone listened to our ideas on how to contact the girl schools. A few were even interested in how our proposal to obtain faculty reports would work out.

I had a special relationship with sophomore Dick Kehoe. Every morning Tom and I would have to walk to the academy, which would take us a half an hour or so. Dick had a new motorcycle. I'm not sure where he lived but he parked it at the academy in the morning. There were several times when my classmate Ken Dempsey, Tom and I wanted to have an early meeting before classes started. It wasn't long before Dick offered to give me a ride to school on the back of his motorcycle. Since I always walked to school with Tom, I would say no. One day we had an early planning meeting scheduled and I agreed to let Dick give me a ride to the academy. Dick showed up on time but Mom asked me to help her do something. I don't even remember what it was.

The point of it was that Dick had to go on to school without me so I could help Mom. Whatever the chore was I got it done and ran to school. When I got to the top of Loras Boulevard and looked down the hill to the academy I saw a big traffic jam right across from school. When I got there, they were putting Dick Kehoe into an ambulance and taking him off. I could not believe what I was seeing and asked God to take care of Dick. When I thought about it, I also thanked him for me not being on that motorcycle. I never asked Mom why she delayed me that day. It took three days for Dick Kehoe to die. We all went to the funeral. Much later I noticed that the Loras Academy annual class "Log" didn't even have a picture of Richard Kehoe. No one outside of Dick's family ever had a chance to know Dick, but God did. That is all that matters until we all see Dick again.

As the student council election came closer, it was obvious to us that we were never going to be able to find a time or way to ask all of our students even something as simple as to vote for us. I couldn't do that at student council meetings even though I had always been a member of the council. Ken Dempsey and I participated in some different student activities but even together it was only a small fraction of what was all going on. Tom and I came up with the idea that what we needed were signs we could hang in the halls so everyone could see them when moving from one class to another. We agreed that that was the answer. I don't know where I got the battery-powered moving signs. We painted them "VOTE FOR JIM GRAHAM FOR CLASS PRES." If I remember right, we had five signs and we hung them in the corridor of all three floors of the academy.

The signs lasted for not much more than an hour. Father Eugene Kutsch, who next year became Loras Academy's first guidance counselor, ordered the signs to be removed. They did their job in that everybody in school knew about the election and had some ideas about what I wanted to get done. The assembly hall election debate was both fun and informative. It never was told to me how many students voted or what the candidate vote counts were. Bob Roth focused his campaign on a proposal to have more boy/girl mixers.

While we all supported that idea, nothing ever happened. When it was all over, Bob Roth was elected our class president.

The Academy's First Guidance Counselor

One of the funniest experiences I had at the academy had to do with the academy's newly implemented student counseling system. I think it was about halfway through the year that the senior class had an opportunity to sign up for guidance counseling. Father Kutsch scheduled counseling sessions with two or more students two days of the week. It just so happened that on the day that my session was scheduled Bob Cardelli and I were scheduled that same afternoon.

Bob Cardelli and I were friends all through high school. There was a time when we were sophomores that Bob was having trouble with his Sacred Heart baseball team. The team had a big guerrilla on the team that was preventing Bob from playing where he wanted to. This was destroying the team spirit. Bob made the mistake of telling me about it. Tom and I went over to the Sacred Heart baseball diamond one afternoon. The team was all assembled and Tom and I announced that we were going to be playing on the team. The guerrilla made the mistake of taking a swing at me. Tom and I both beat him up. We would not let him go home. So he had to sit on the sidelines to watch the team play. When the game practice was over, we told the guerrilla we would be back again tomorrow if he did not let Bob Cardelli play and direct the team. As it turned out, Sacred Heart won their league championship.

Bob Cardelli and I showed up for our guidance counseling on the same morning. Bob went first. A half an hour later he came out shaking his head in disbelief. We talked a little, and he told me that Father Kutch had advised him that college would be hard for Bob and that he should keep his eyes open for opportunities in the job world. I asked Bob to wait until I was finished and we would talk about it. I walked in the room and saw that it was organized about the same way as it was with my meeting as a sophomore with our principal Father O'Brien. I sat in the chair in front of his desk. He began to explain what he thought my strengths were. He thought I would get along fine in the community even if I did not go to college.

He asked if I had any post high school plans. I told him I had not really made up my mind, just to see what he would say. He then explained several career opportunities. He told me not to worry about it and wished me good luck. When I got outside the room I compared notes with Bob Cardelli and we started to laugh. I don't know what made it so funny but I may not have laughed any harder in my life. We heard Father Kutch coming out of the room. We got a head start running down the hall laughing all the way before he even got to the door. Bob Cardelli became a medical doctor. We both finished Loras College four years later. I last met Bob Cardelli in Iowa City when he was in medical school and I was in law school.

I'll never be able to thank my mother and dad enough for sending us to Loras Academy. Dad knew what he was doing because he graduated from the same school even though it was no longer called Columbia Academy.

CHAPTER 4—IN THE ARMY NOW

Fort Leonard Wood, Missouri

When I graduated from Loras Academy everybody was subject to the possibility of being drafted into the army for a two-year term. I had decided that I could not be who I was intended to be if I did not have a college degree. Of course my intent was to go to Loras College. At this time the army had a six-month-active-duty and five-year-reserve training program. The more I looked into this the more sense it seemed to make. The program that was available in Dubuque was tied to the 389th Engineering Battalion, which was headquartered in Dubuque. Because of this, my five-year reserve training time would be spent right in Dubuque. This was the best of all worlds. I could go to college while living at home and make money with monthly army meetings and summer army engineering training programs. I wasn't thinking about how hard it might be to get my bachelor's degree in three and half years in order to stay on schedule with the rest of my class.

Both basic training and advance construction equipment training was provided a couple of hundred miles away at Fort Leonard Wood, Missouri. Basic training was a new challenge. When I first arrived at Fort Leonard Wood, we were all assigned to one of five two-story barracks sleeping quarters. There were twelve bunks on both sides of the first floor and twelve bunks on both sides of the second floor. Everyone had a bunk and a foot locker in the center aisle at the foot of his bed to keep his clothes and uniforms in. There were young guys from a dozen states all packed in together and all wondering what was going to happen. In our first meeting we all lined up in four rows in front of the building and the sergeant in command of us started to ask the group what their military experience was.

There was one guy who told the sergeant he was the commanding general in an ROTC program someplace in another state. It became clear to me that he was looking to be selected as barracks leader. He seemed to be arrogant and if that were true and he was selected as barracks leader and he knew about my leadership skills, the next ninety days would not be good for me. I kept my mouth shut. He was selected as what they called our *guide arm*. What that meant was that he carried our company's flag when we marched everywhere.

The physical training was hard but no big deal. The first problem in our barracks company was that there were four or five guys who needed schooling or help to master basic marching and organizational skills. Our guide arm leader did nothing to help except yell at them. That meant that two people were yelling at these four or five guys all day long. In order to inject some sanity into the day, I talked two guys into helping me show and help these trainees know how to do what they needed to do. They learned quickly and everybody stopped yelling, except for special occasions when we screwed something up.

We had some neat guys in our barracks. One of the guys who helped me was Tom Dempsey. Tom came from Oshkosh, Wisconsin. He, too, had the benefit of a high school ROTC program. Tom, two others in our barracks, and I were in the squad leaders. I don't remember the names of the other two squad leaders. As squad leaders, we worked together and helped one another at whatever we were doing. There was one other special guy named Larry Justus. Larry was a perfect specimen of a muscled superstar. He took really good care of himself and even did more exercise than what we were required to. The problem with Larry Justus was that he never said a single word. He still could be counted on to help and lead, even though he never said anything.

After we had been in training for a month, the focus changed from our training as individuals to a contest between our barracks and the other four barracks at the camp. This was where things really got interesting. Our barracks was awarded first place really early in the judging. After that all we ever heard about was how we were going to stay first. It really wasn't all that hard. Everybody knew what they were doing and we worked together, even though Mr. Flag (our guide arm) took all the credit for it. It was just a matter of time before there would be a reckoning between myself and Mr. Flag. One day I walked into the barracks when there was almost no one else there. Mr. Flag and two of his bigger slaves stood in front of me. Mr. Flag told me that this was the time that I was to learn who the leader of this barracks was.

Unknown to Mr. Flag and to me, Larry Justus was sleeping on the bottom bunk ten feet away. Larry never moved. He just laid there and said: "I would not do that if I were you." The two thugs knew if they entered the fight they would die. That left Mr. Flag and me alone. Mr. Flag was taller and bigger than me but he was slower than me. All I had to do was wait until he threw the first punch, block it, and smack him squarely in the jaw. My second, third and fourth punches were all in the face. He never really had a chance. When it was over he ended up with a split lip, a closed eye and a very sore stomach. I probably went too far but I was doing this not just for me but for everybody in the barracks. The next morning when we were outside in formation our sergeant asked him what happened. He didn't say anything for a couple of seconds, and then told the sergeant that he had fallen down the stairs. For the rest of our training, Mr. Flag carried the flag but nobody paid any attention to him.

The contest between us and the other four barracks never ended. Supposedly the last event was a twenty-mile march in full gear. It should have been called a twenty-mile race in full gear. By this time, everyone in our barracks was in great physical shape and we were proud of it. We took out the map and figured out where common sense required us to stop and rest so that we all got to the destination together. If we were not there together it would not count. We redistributed some of our weight to our stronger soldiers. The winner of this exercise would theoretically qualify for a free weekend leave. Besides that, the winner would likely be named the best platoon for the summer. The whole thing went as planned until we got about halfway. At that point everyone slept for twenty minutes and ate whatever we carried with us. The food was mostly candy, energy food and water. No one had to yell at anyone. Some of us carried two rifles before it was over. Our barracks not only made it we finished first.

We arrived at the finish line a full hour before any other barracks did. However, it didn't turn out the way we thought it would. Despite our win, the commanding officer refused to designate us as the Best Platoon based solely on the twenty-mile march. The next day we were informed that the winner of a two-mile race that was to be run a week from then would be the Best Platoon. It didn't matter to us. We knew we were the Best Platoon. We were informed that the first platoon that got its forty-eight members across the finish line would win the race. Tom Dempsey and I were good runners. We had two other guys who were sprinters for their high-school track team. Everyone else in our barracks was in *really* good shape. The game plan was simple. We would run in pairs of two to protect one another and encourage one another. Once we got to within a hundred yards of the finish line, everyone was to give it their absolute best.

On the day of the race all five platoons gathered together at the beginning line. We had about an hour to meet and talk to one another before the race began. We were concerned about two guys we knew were high-school distance runners from one of the other barracks. Maybe they could make us look bad by finishing way ahead of everyone and force us to go through a third contest to win best platoon.

Everybody in all of the other four barracks knew of Larry Justus, even though they may not have worked alongside of him. Larry walked over to these two distance runners and I saw him point me out. I later found out that Larry told the two distance runners that it was not in their best interest to finish the race before me. As we got a hundred yards from the finish line, I saw that one of the two runners was only ten yards behind me. I still had something left and gave it my best. Our barracks won the race! Maybe the second best thing that happened that day was that Mr. Flag redeemed himself when he finished in the top 10 from our platoon.

We earned a three-day pass and could leave the base to enjoy it. It was then that I made my first big mistake. I agreed to go with Larry Justus on our out-of-post visit to St. Louis; neither one of us had ever been there before. After we got off the bus downtown and started looking around Larry had an idea. He talked me into walking twenty feet ahead of him while walking down the sidewalk downtown. I had no idea what he was up to but as long as we were together I felt safe. As I was walking by two guys jumped out of an alley, grabbed me and pulled me into the alley.

They told me to give them my wallet and said they would kill me if I didn't. I reached for my wallet and tried to delay for a couple seconds until Larry showed up. One punch by Larry in the back of the first guy's head dropped the biggest guy, and Larry finished off the guy I was working with. Larry and I took their wallets and everything that was in them. Then we removed their shirts, pants, underwear and shoes. We walked a couple of blocks and put all that stuff down the street drain. I thanked God I was still alive and tried to enjoy seeing and doing all the stuff that we did. Sometime later, I wondered if these two guys filed a police record. I laughed when I wondered if it included an entry called INDECENT EXPOSURE. The more I thought about this whole event, I decided that this was the last time I was going to go on a pass with Larry Justus.

After basic training I spent four months learning how to operate bulldozers, graders, and dozer-pulled dirt scrapers. This was the biggest construction equipment the army had. It was not easy but it was very interesting. It really paid off to help me make a contribution while working with the 389th Engineering Battalion later in Dubuque.

Camp McCoy, Wisconsin—389th Engineering Battalion

I was not the only high-school graduate of the class of 1956 to choose six months' active duty and five years' active reserves and thus avoid the possibility of a two-year draft. I can't remember how many soldiers there were in the battalion. It was something like sixty or seventy. Several of us had heavy equipment training. I can't remember if Dick Blasen was part of the battalion before I got there or if he came about the same time I did. Dick and I were friends all through Saint Columbkille grade school. We were in the same class and did everything together. We knew and trusted one another. John Ryan was also in the battalion. John and I were never really apart all four years at Loras Academy. John was a squad leader on the academy's unbelievably successful drill team. A year later my brother Tom came to the 389th Engineering Battalion and fit right in. All four of us started as privates and quickly earned promotion.

Dubuque's 389th Engineering Battalion was led by officers Frank Richardson and Bob Burgmeier. If I remember right, Captain Richardson had an engineering and land surveying background. While Captain Richardson's background contributed to our success, his real strength was in the building a multi skilled team. Like most officers, he relied on written and visual text on how-you-do-it training. This was basically what we were doing all through my freshman year at Loras College. We had a pretty good core of people who knew how to operate and maintain heavy equipment, trucks, gasoline tankers and jack hammers. We even had two guys who knew something about how to set up and use dynamite.

The battalion had two weaknesses. The first was we were a relatively new and inexperienced group. The second was that we had never led a big construction project. The Army Corp of Engineers headquarters was always demanding training progress papers and statistics. They used this information to determine how we would be used in summer camp engineering construction exercises. For a long time, the 389th Engineering Battalion wasn't big enough to be assigned a summer construction project on its own. The 389th was thus blended in with another organization and got little or no credit for whatever was done other than a record that we had participated in it. Our officers Captain Richardson and Bob Burgmeier solved this problem. They faithfully recorded and reported the growth of our membership and the scope of our training.

Our First Sergeant, Ronald Hagenstein, was a real key to any success we were going to have. As we went through the training, he would ask us what we would do if the equipment we saw in the film broke down. Then whether he liked the answer or not we would go to the bulldozer or grader and Sgt. Hagenstein would require us to point out the problem and explain the solution.

Then it got worse. He would have us take the problem part off the machine, check it out, and then reinstall it. In six months or so everybody knew their assignment and they were confident in their ability to do it. About the beginning of my sophomore year, Sgt. Hagenstein added a new wrinkle to the problem. The question became, if the equipment breaks down where do you find the replacement and how do you get the replacement on the job to avoid disrupting the entire construction process? It did not take very long for anyone to realize that the answers to these problems were going to make the difference between success and failure for the time-constrained construction projects that our growing battalion was likely to be assigned to.

For the first time, everyone was tied into what was needed to make it possible for us to succeed. This was not an academic problem because we all were sure that we were going to be assigned a construction project at Camp McCoy, Wisconsin, this summer. Everyone in the company, including the officers, got together to solve these problems. We looked at it from the big picture to figure out what physical resources were needed and how to assign work details so that we were working long enough and hard enough to get the job done on time. We considered breakdown backup resources from two points of view. We needed backup equipment and not *just* the ability to make short-term repairs. The other key to success was the development of work schedules so people remained alert while they were operating the equipment. Losing a piece of equipment or an operator to fatigue was not acceptable and could well lead to project failure. Ambulance and equipment removal needs could lose a half a day when all we had was a month to succeed.

When we actually received the announcement that we were going to have our own project at Camp McCoy, I and two other soldiers had just made the rank of sergeant. We had ninety days to get ready. We thought we were ready. In order to better plan for the project Capt. Richardson and Sgt. Hagenstein visited our project at Camp McCoy. What they discovered was not good. We had to build a five-mile stretch of basically a two-lane rural road. The problem was not the length of the road. It was the fact that we had to carve our way through a rock hill about an eighth of a mile long in the middle of the project.

When our officers and sergeants got together to plan, it was clear that if we worked from one end of the project to the other end it would take more than a month to complete the work on time. This was true even if we worked twelve-hour days. We had to break our equipment up so that we were working on both sides of the hill that we had to blast through. No work could be done near the blast area to establish a finish grade and shape to the road nor could we build entrance and exit points in that eight-mile stretch to and from the road until the blasting was completed. It also meant that the finished road construction work had to be done simultaneously on both sides of the blasting area.

At this point, our non-commissioned officer leadership group made several basic decisions. Each piece of equipment would have two operators. Each operator would work half of the day. This way no one would work more than four hours without a four-hour break. Work would begin at dawn and stop at dusk on the open areas where no dynamite rock removal was required. Our survey team would stake every work area as soon as each phase of the work was completed so that its completion could be proven. In order to have any chance of finishing opening the road through the rock hill it was necessary to have gas-operated floodlights, so that rock-busting jackhammering could be completed at night. This also allowed dynamite to be set up at night as needed to be able to loosen and remove rock for the next day. This worked out well. No dynamite was lit until dawn the next day. When the dynamite went off, every one woke up whether they wanted to or not.

When we got to our equipment, we found that it was already gassed up and ready to go. Gassing up the equipment was a story in itself. We figured we could not get standard gas trucks into several hard-to-reach areas. This meant there were bound to be equipment downtimes. In order to be able to bring diesel fuel right to the equipment where it was working, we designed a rack to hold a fifty-gallon diesel-fuel drum on the back of two four-wheel-drive three-quarter-ton trucks. That way, we could take the fuel to the equipment and loose no work time. The three-quarter-ton trucks were ready to go on the first day we got to the base.

No one stayed at any barracks. We all camped out in the same woods where we parked the trucks, backup equipment and the mess tents for our cooks. Dick Blasen and I slept in the same pup tent right next to one of our backup deuce-and-a-half dump trucks. Capt. Richardson, Bob Burgmeier and Sgt. Hagenstein used a bigger tent near the mess tent.

Things went really well the first two weeks. We had very little rain and almost no equipment delays. Our dynamite work was on schedule or maybe a little bit ahead of schedule. A lot of the rock we took out of the hill we trucked to and used to build a base underneath several other parts of the road. Our short four-hour rotating equipment operator work schedule really kept our equipment working at full capacity all the time. Just as we planned, we had to remove and replace one of the big bulldozers and do extensive repair work on a bulldozer-pulled dirt removing scraper.

What we were not counting on was nature, or more specifically, animal nature. Around midnight two and a half weeks into the project, Dick Blasen and I were sound asleep in our pup tent. During the night Dick was bit on the ear by what was obviously a rabid skunk. Dick's head was no more than six inches from my head when the skunk bit him. We both got out of the tent in an instant. I sounded the warning and someone killed the skunk with a shovel. Dick's ear was torn and it bled a lot. Capt. Richardson used his field phone to call for an ambulance. Dick and the dead skunk left for the army's Great Lakes Hospital within an hour. My brother Tom and I drove up to Great Lakes to visit Dick after our campout was completed. We laughed about it, but it was not all that funny at the time. While Dick ended up no worse for the wear, it changed everything at the camp. Instead of sleeping on the ground, we raised the dump truck beds so that water would run out if it rained. We slept in them or in the cabs of the spare equipment.

Things worked out even better than we had hoped and planned for the project. When we got to the point where there was only ten days left, we knew we were going to be finished three or maybe four days before the deadline. Our daily status report system and equipment maintenance planning made it possible to adjust whatever we had to adjust from day to day without the loss of any time or work. At this point, I tried to talk Sgt. Hagenstein into using one of our three-quarter-ton trucks to go into town and buy all of the beer it could hold so we could at least enjoy the evenings of the last couple of days. He told me that he did not want to hear anything about it! The next day I met the equipment operators as they came back from their shifts and told them what I had planned to do. Everyone thought that was a good idea. I collected more money than I remember. The next day, I think it was, John Ryan and I went into town and came back with a full truck, the contents of which we hid DEEP in the woods.

Then something happened I could not control. Capt. Richardson came up to me when the day's work was done and I was eating dinner. He told me that Camp McCoy was going to have a best soldier contest. Each of the three battalions working on their separate projects was directed to send one soldier to the base headquarters to compete in their best soldier contest. I tried to talk my way out of it and suggested two or three others who would be better contestants, but it did not work. I ended up going to the base PX grocery store and buying brass polish and shoe polish and using someone else's iron to iron my uniform. While all this was going on, I thought about Tom and John Ryan and the other guys drinking my beer. The contest itself was kind of a farce. Here is where my Loras Academy drill team, rifle team, company commander, and student council activities really paid off.

It was not even close. I still have the twelve-inch shiny brass trophy. It says:

305th ENGR GPs
BEST SOLDIER 1958 AUT
SGT. JAMES E. GRAHAM
CO. "B" 389 BN

Looking back at this now, I realize how useful this wonderful military leadership training was. The key to anything in life is not just desire, opportunity and luck. Nor is it just tenacity. At this point in my life I knew I had Graham tenacity. I also found out that success requires knowing what can go wrong and being ready to deal with it if and when it does.

I don't know what happened to our Best Company trophy. I hope Captain Richardson gave it to his kids. The last Christmas card we received from Anne Richardson, Captain Richardson's wife, was from Fort Meyers Beach, Florida in 2010.

CHAPTER 5—LIFE AT FRENTRESS LAKE COTTAGES, A HISTORY

Both the Graham and Schiltz family have a long history of playing at Frentress Lake. My grandfather, Edward Graham, and his family may have had one of the original cottages on the Lake. My father, Joseph Graham, his brother, Father John Graham and Dad's three sisters Irene, Patricia and Marie all grew up on the Mississippi River at Frentress Lake in the 1920s and '30s. This continued until Grandpa Graham sold his cottage and bought his farm on Cedar Cross Road southwest of Dubuque, where my brother Tom and I had so much fun.

My grandfather, Harry Schiltz's father and family had a cottage at Frentress Lake in the same 1920s and '30s time frame. The Schiltz cottage was not located on the east or on the Illinois side of Frentress Lake where all the cottages now are. Grandpa Schiltz's cottage was located on what is now an island that is the west side of the lake. When Grandpa Schiltz's cottage was built, the Mississippi River had not yet been dammed. Once the river was dammed, river water levels rose to the point where you could no longer get to the Schiltz cottage. All that remains of the Schiltz cottage is some cement work on the south side of the lake island and a black-and-white picture of the cottage that my wife Jane restored. It remains in the Graham cottage to this date.

I think my father bought his Frentress Lake cottage in 1950. One of my first memories of our cottage was digging a large hole in the hot afternoon sun for a septic tank next to the cottage between it and the river. The cottage next door north was owned by Jim and Barbara Klinger. It was Mrs. Klinger who brought me some ice water when I was near the end of digging the big septic tank hole. My mother and Barbara Klinger were classmates at Clark College in Dubuque. Sometime later the cottage south of Dad's was also owned by Mom's sister, Elizabeth Jane [Betty] Kuehnle. Betty's cottage is now owned by Betty's daughter Mary T. Lyons and her husband, Dan. This was a wonderful place for all of us boys to live and spend our summers.

Frentress Lake was a place where we could explore nature one wonderful day after another. At the north end of the lake there were two older men who caught and sold catfish in big six-foot-long, two-foot-square, wooden lath traps. At one end of the trap, there were fingers of narrow wood lath that all pointed into the middle of the trap. A catfish would swim into the trap and spread the lath fingers in order to get to the food at the back of the trap. Then the lath would close in on the fish so it could not get out. It was so simple and yet so genius. When Tom and I found out they were retiring, we asked them if we could have one of their catfish traps, and they gave it to us.

It took Tom and me a couple of days to wander up and down the waters of the islands between Frentress Lake and the Mississippi River to find the deepest hole to put the trap in so we could catch a big, big, catfish. That was what the two fishermen told us we needed to do if we wanted to catch BIG fish.

Tom and I found the deepest hole there was in the river back waters west of Frentress Lake and checked our trap for a couple of days. We kept adding bait to it as we checked the trap. We got to thinking that if we catch any huge catfish it would be hard to lift and pull the trap into our aluminum flat boat. Our second thought was how to keep a big fish from breaking up the trap once we got the trap into the boat. We figured that between the two of us we would be strong enough to get the trap into the boat. We took Dad's .22 rifle with us to kill the fish and save the trap.

The next time we got to our deep hole to check the trap we noticed that the trap was *really* heavy. We looked at one another and knew that we had caught our trophy catfish! We took a deep breath and pulled the trap onto the bottom of the boat. The trap was no sooner in the boat when the huge fish made one big flap and broke the trap into several pieces. That was not the worst of it. The catfish knocked Tom down, twice! Tom got up mad, grabbed the .22 and shot the huge catfish three times. That quieted the catfish, but it also put three holes in the boat. I drove back to the cottage and Tom plugged the holes with his fingers so the boat did not fill up with water. We never told Dad about the holes. We just fixed them with some tar and pop rivets. We spent all morning cleaning the fish and cutting it into pieces small enough to cook and eat. We saved the head and mounted it on a tree so everyone could see it.

While we could catch fish off of the Graham boat dock any time we wanted to—and we did a lot—there was one other fishing experience that, to this day, I still think is hard for other people to believe. One summer Tom and I built a small eight-foot-long, flat-bottomed, light-plywood boat that we raced around the lake with our 7.5-horsepower Elgin outboard motor. The motor wasn't all that strong but the boat was light. We thought we were flying. The key to its speed was that it only sat in the water about two inches. One day when we were riding from our house at 135 South Hill Street in Dubuque, Iowa, to the cottage on the Illinois side of the river we drove by the long lake or back water just south of East Dubuque. From the road it looked like there was no way to get into the lake to fish. Tom and I asked around about it and found out that it was called Lake Locoma. We were told that it was in fact land locked. We figured that if we got into it we might be the first persons to ever fish it. There had to be some connection between the river and the lake. Maybe we could drag our little boat across the land to get to the lake.

We must've had twenty-five dozen night crawlers when we took off to find a way to fish it. When we got next to the lake we rode north along the riverside looking for a way into the landlocked lake. The best we could come up with was what looked to be a stream or low water path from the riverside east across the tree-covered ground to the lake. There was only six or eight inches of water in the waterway and the waterway was only a foot wider than our boat. Tom and I had to get out of the boat and push and pull it across the water path to the lake. It all worked out fine until we got to the lake and tried to get back into the boat. We discovered that our legs and feet were covered with maybe as many as twenty leeches! We helped one another pull the leeches off and got into the boat to fish. We spent almost the entire day catching catfish. It didn't take us long to figure out we only needed half of a night crawler to catch a catfish. Then we went to a fourth of a night crawler when it was clear we were running out of bait. We should have kept the leeches for bait! That was the best fishing I ever had.

When Tom and I were not using our little, plywood flat boat, little brother Joe would. Dad would fill up the Elgin's small gas tank in the morning and let little Joe run the boat around in big circles in front of the cottage where Dad could watch him until he ran out of gas and had to paddle the boat to shore. It did not take much gas for Joe to do that, and Joe never missed an opportunity to do it.

Dad also never missed an opportunity to sit on the picnic table and feed the ducks. There was not a duck on the whole lake that did not take advantage of Dad's corn seed distribution every morning. Tom and I would stop our fishing or whatever we were doing while Dad was taking care of the ducks. At night, Mom, Dad, Tom and I, and maybe a neighbor or two, would play poker. Poker was a good card game. Playing with Mom and Dad taught Tom and me that you could not always believe what the other player was saying or betting.

One of Dad's sayings stuck with me all my life. If Tom or I made a bad bet and Dad thought that we should have known better, he would call us "A STUTE." It was one thing to call Tom and me "A STUTE" but he also called anyone who made a mistake when he or she was playing with us the same thing. We knew what he meant but it took a while for other people to catch on. Poker was a great game. It was not only fun to play but once in a while you even learned something about cards and people. I was never all that lucky at getting cards in poker but Tom was the luckiest poker player I ever knew.

I remember when we were in high school at Loras Academy, Tom and I started the neighborhood version of what now everyone calls "King of the Dock." We'd play in the evening or on especially hot days or on holidays like the Fourth of July when all of our relatives and all our lake neighbor kids would gather at Dad's dock. It started out as an excuse to be thrown into the water off the dock to cool off. It did not take long for the little kids to try to gang up on Tom and me. As the kids grew up it became harder to prevent them from throwing Tom and me in the water. This started as a generational thing and it still is. Once this nonsense got started it would sometimes last for a couple of hours until everyone just wore out. Several years ago, Jane took a wonderful photo of all of this nonsense that still hangs in what is now my brother Joe Graham's new cottage. But that's another story. It's not just a cottage anymore. It is a gathering place for the whole Graham family. More on this subject later.

CHAPTER 6—LORAS COLLEGE WAS A GOOD TIME

C lasses at Loras College were not all that hard. The texts were good and the instructors not only cared but were really good at what they did. My problem was that I always had to take an extra class and sometimes two classes in order to make up classes that I could not take when I was in the military on active duty for six months. I noted when I first started class in the second semester of my freshman year that Father Eugene Kutch was the College Dean of Men, or student enforcer. I did not think I would have any trouble with Father Kutch and I didn't.

Once in a while, I found myself in a class that was required for graduation. Nobody really wanted to be in it and nobody worked really hard at it. Spanish was this class for me. I took only one year of Spanish at Loras Academy and had to have a second year of Spanish in order to meet Loras College's graduation requirements. The teacher, Mr. LeBlanc, I think, tried his best to make the class interesting. The text was not merely mechanical how to do it. It also contained short stories and a poem or two. I wondered how the professor was going to figure out who got the B's and the A's in the class. One Monday morning he assigned a love poem to everyone and told us that he would give everyone an opportunity to recite it on Friday. I knew right then that the poem would determine if anyone got an A in the class. The next Friday I was ready. The professor called everyone in our alphabetical order to recite the poem.

When it was my turn, I knelt on one knee in front of the desk of the ugliest kid in the class and recited the poem while looking him in the eye. With as much passion as I could muster, I spoke softly as I stared at him. I slowly waved my hands petitioning him to hear and believe me as I spoke. The poem was pretty long. About halfway through I wiped my eyes to wipe away my tears. He couldn't' believe what was happening and was really glad when I finished and stood up again.

Everyone had blank expressions, that is, everyone except Tom Yates, who lived north of Dodge Street on my way to both Loras Academy and later Loras College. Tom Yates and I worked with one another for four years in high school. He put two and two together and he too figured out that this was the tiebreaker. He had more than a half an hour to mentally prepare himself. That was his advantage because his last name was Yates. He did a good job but it was not polished like my presentation. I got the only A. Tom got the only B in the class.

Skinning the Raccoon

While I was in service on active duty at Fort Leonard Wood, Missouri, I could occasionally return home to Dubuque on weekends. At that time I was still dating Kathleen Zwack. Kathleen was a junior at the Visitation Academy. Her brother, Joe Zwack, was a year behind me in my brother Tom's class. The Zwacks were a nice family. Kathleen's father was killed in World War II. Kathleen and her two little sisters, Margo and Ellen, and their mother lived with her mother's parents, Mr. and Mrs. Kie, if I remember the name right. Kathleen was very social. When I would get back from Fort Leonard Wood, we went to every dance and every social event I could. However, there soon came a time when I could no longer keep up with her schedule. The more times I missed or couldn't make something, the more agitated she got. It was clear to me that I needed to break off my relationship with Kathleen. I had to find an innocent way to do it. I did not want to hurt her or anyone in her family.

One Saturday after I was back in Dubuque for good, it was a beautiful sunshiny fall day. I needed just to get away from things. I took my shotgun and drove five or six miles north of Dubuque into some sunny, hilly woods where I liked to squirrel hunt. I found the perfect spot in a little wooded valley where I could see in two directions. Then I made the mistake of sitting down and leaning against a tree. I am sure that it was not five minutes before I fell asleep with the sun on my face. When I woke up, ten yards away from me there was this huge raccoon coming down a big tree head first and looking right at me. I had an idea. Before the raccoon could take another step, I shot him. I knew that my hunting day was done so I picked up the raccoon and put him in the trunk of the car. As I drove to Kathleen's house, I wondered how to do this. I knew her whole family was likely to be home. I decided to drive up the alley behind her house and park near their back door.

I ran up to the back door. With an excited voice I called: "Hey, everyone, look what I've got!" Kathleen, her brother Joe, and her mother came out of the house and went down to the car. Her grandparents also came out of the house but stayed on the porch. I told Kathleen and everyone that I had always had the most wonderful idea that I never dreamed would ever come true. I opened the trunk, held up the big, dead, somewhat-bloody raccoon and showed it to everyone. I told Kathleen that I had shot the most beautiful raccoon I had ever seen. I told her I intended to make a coonskin cap out of it. I asked Kathleen if she would help me clean and skin the raccoon. You should have seen the expression on Kathleen's face! She could not believe what I had asked her to do. She started screaming at me: "You are awful! I NEVER want to see you again!" As this was going on, I looked up at the porch and saw her grandparents smiling at one another as they walked back into the house. That was the last time I dated Kathleen. I rode home with a smile on my face and buried the wonderful raccoon in our backyard at 135 South Hill Street.

One More Try at Dating

There was one other dating event that I remember with a smile when I was a sophomore at Loras College. There was, and still is, an ice rink two blocks west of Kane Hall where a lot of people ice-skated every afternoon and early evening. My friend John Ryan, my brother Tom and I would bring our ice skates and hockey sticks to play on Tuesdays and Thursdays after our two o'clock class. John Ryan, Tom, and I were all part of the 389th Engineering Battalion. We were not only going to school together we also went to the army-reserve meetings together. One afternoon I noticed there was a beautiful girl just skating quietly on the rink. I asked John Ryan and some other kids what they knew about her. They told me that her name was Joan Allen and that she was very private and would not talk to anyone. I knew how to deal with that problem.

We started playing hockey. It wasn't long before we were not just passing the puck back and forth to one another but we had some real speed built up. As John Ryan passed me the puck, I flashed in front of Joan Allen, fell down and slid close to her. I didn't move for a minute. She came up and asked: "Are you all right?" I didn't say anything for a second or two. Finally I told her: "I think I am." I asked her what her name was. She told me her name Joan Allen and we talked. We met one another at the ice rink a couple times after that before I invited her to come to our house for a dance party in our beautiful basement. Tom invited Cathy Meyer and four or five other couples. We all had a wonderful time. Soon thereafter, Tom met Mary Green, who was a neighbor of Joan's. Mary Green lived east and across the street from Joan. We all double dated for a couple of months until the girls got too serious and it didn't work out.

In Tom's case, I remember when the four of us were coming home from a dance. I was parked at the curb while Tom took Mary Green thirty feet away up on her front porch. They stopped and Tom gave Mary a hug. Mary said firmly: "Hold me tighter!" Tom said, "If I hold you any tighter I will break your bra." The next sound we heard was Mary slapping Tom. Joan and I busted out laughing when we heard the slap. After Tom got back into the car, I took Joan to her home a couple of houses up the street.

The next week Joan and I were going to a dance. I knocked on her door and walked into the living room. There was no one there. Joan called from upstairs. She said: "I will be down in a minute." I sat and waited in the living room. A few minutes later she started to walk down the stairs. I saw that she had next to nothing on. I may be stupid but I knew where this was going to go. I ran for my life out the front door.

The Ugliest Girl in Dubuque Contest

Between college and army reserve meetings there really wasn't much time to do anything during the school year. About the only time we ever got together at Loras College was in the school cafeteria where we would meet, have a little lunch, a Coke and talk. The talk sooner or later got to be focused on girls. At that time, Loras College was a school for men only. The cafeteria was a good place to meet. It was a big room full of tables so that you can always find a semiprivate table to talk. After a short conversation about the school or classes, our talk always turned to girls. It was a lot of fun relating the conversations we each had with our respective girlfriends.

One day we had an idea. I want to think it was my brother Tom who came up with the idea but he might now deny it. I guess if it was not Tom it must've been me. It went like this. Since we were having trouble keeping track of and remembering the names of the girls who were nothing but trouble, we thought we should come up with a jingle that would help us remember them. The jingle would help us remember who these girls were and thus help all of us avoid making the same mistake twice.

This was truly a fun time for us. We told one another of all of our experiences with girls. We recorded the names of all the girls we agreed deserved to become part of our jingle. In order to remind ourselves of the purpose of this effort, we spent some time trying to decide how we should title the jingle. We must have gone through a dozen potential titles until we finally settled on a one that reminded us of our purpose in doing this. At the same time, it was simple enough to always remember.

We decided that the jingle would simply be called "The Ugliest Girl in Dubuque." That decision came rather easily. The more we thought about it, it was apparent that some candidates on the list were more deserving of this recognition than were other candidates. Our sense of justice required that we also rank the girls who made the list in the order of their importance. The list itself was relatively easy to come up with. It included the nine best qualified. The girls who made this list made the list not because they were not good looking. Does that make any sense?

They made the list because they just could not be depended upon, they did not have a reasonable sense of humor, or worse, they had their own agenda concerning where they wanted to go and what they wanted to do. I have been advised not to use their actual names in writing the *South Hill Rascals*. What must be understood at this point was that no malice was ever intended in us going through this exercise. None of us were thinking about the consequences of us doing this. To get on with it, the jingle went this way. Remember this includes nine girls and one girl twice because she was a consensus choice. It went like this:

"Ri-Bo-See See-Cle-Clo-Lu-Mor-Mud-Rose-Aline-Kringle."

This was all supposed to be private conversations between us guys. The mistake we made was not that we were laughing so hard when we were doing this. It was that we could not make up our minds on how the girls should be ranked on the list. What we decided to do was to put these abbreviations on the board without any clarifying information so that we all had a chance to think about it before our next meeting knowing what their present ranking was.

Somehow, someone found out what we were doing and the purpose behind the bulletin board information. I suppose this was to be expected but what happened next was unjust and unreasonable. Someone told the girls at Clark College what this was all about. The next day a dozen girls from Clark College invaded the Loras lunchroom and tore the note off the bulletin board. Some of the girls gave speeches about how disgusting, mean and rotten this was. Neither my brother Tom, John Ryan, nor I were there when all of this happened, but we heard about it. After that, I don't think I had a date until I was a senior. That was all right because I sure had plenty to do.

This subject came up again many years later when my wife, Jane, and I attended the fifty-year celebration of my graduation from Loras College. A good time was had by all. I got a chance to see John Ryan again, Fay Chapman and many other classmates I had not seen since our Loras College graduation. Lo and behold, John Ahern, Tom and my former grade school Boy Scout leader served as one of the after-dinner program moderators. I found out that John Ahern did join the Marines and then came back to Dubuque to graduate in my class at Loras College. The old Boy Scout history never came up.

I was one of several classmates who gave a little storytelling speech. I told the class and their wives the "Ugliest Girl in Dubuque" story. Most of my classmates did not know anything about it and had never heard the story before. You could not believe the expression on the faces of their wives as I told it. Their husbands knew they had to keep their mouths shut or they would die. When I finished the story some of the Loras Academy classmates who knew me all busted out laughing. Everyone else had puzzled expressions and their wives could have been momentarily offended. My wife overheard one of the wives of someone say: "No wonder he had no dates for two years! That was a penalty that he deserved! If I had gotten a call from him, my response would have been an immediate *CLICK!*" I couldn't help myself. I busted out laughing.

Our Adopted Brother Ernest (Ernie) Garthwaite

Ernie was in my class at Loras College. I don't really remember how we met. I liked Ernie from the start. I found out that both of his parents were killed in an automobile accident in Canada. I studied economics and other things but Ernie studied art. I really did not blame him because Loras had a priest who was a renowned art instructor at the time. Ernie had a good sense of humor and we invited him home to meet Mom and Dad. Things turned out so well that Ernie ate at home with us at least three times a week. Being an artist, Ernie could not resist painting a mural on our South Hill Street basement wall where Tom, Ernie, and I had our girlfriends over to dance and sing and enjoy other nonsense, including Mom's ice cream and cake. Before the evening was over, we got to know Ernie pretty well and invited him to the cottage in the summer. I guess you could say that Ernie was our adopted brother.

Shortly after I graduated from the University of Iowa law school, my father sold our house at 135 South Hill Street to Jerry (Bud) Noonan and his wife, Lola. He did this in order to build the Graham Style Store, then a men's clothing store, on the corner of Eighth and Main Street in downtown Dubuque. In a recent visit with the Noonans, they remembered and reminded us that Ernie Garthwaite had painted two pictures in the basement of our house. The first scene was a picture of Beetle Bailey with some dialogue. The second scene was a small Elvis Presley with his guitar.

About halfway through my sophomore year, or maybe it was the beginning of my junior year, Ernie started to have trouble at

Loras College. The source of the problem was three students from Chicago. I don't know if Ernie had expressed an interest in one of their Chicago girlfriends who was attending Clark College or not. It didn't really matter until one of the Chicago guys punched Ernie in the face. That night at dinner, Tom and I had a hard time getting Ernie to tell us what happened. We finally succeeded. He knew the names of the three guys. I knew that at least one of them lived in Kane Hall. Ernie thought that two of them lived together in Kane Hall. We decided we would go visit them.

It was a relatively simple plan. I would knock on the door and take the first guy on. Tom would wait on the side of the door and take the second guy if he showed up from the side. This way, we would maintain the element of surprise and get it over quickly so we could get out of Kane Hall before we got into trouble. It went pretty much the way we planned. I knocked and one of the three guys came to the door. I told him why we were there and watched while he was making up his mind what to do. As planned, he took the first shot and I blocked the punch. Three punches later he was on the floor. I went to the door and asked for the other guy and found out that he was not there. I asked where he lived from whoever was there. He told me he did not know. I asked the same thing of the third guy and got the same answer. Tom and I looked at one another and left.

Ernie never had any more trouble. We stayed together and played together until Ernie and I graduated from Loras College and went our own ways. Ernie made several trips back to Loras College but either I never knew about them until it was too late or I simply couldn't get there. Forty years later, we connected again. Every time I think of Ernie it brings a smile to my face.

That happens a lot, as Jane and I have two beautiful paintings by Ernie in our home that we see every day. Ernie is also special to the whole Graham family. My brother Joe has kept Ernie's big portrait of Mom and Dad and us four boys at his brand-new Frentress Lake cottage. Every time we visit Dubuque for our Fourth of July family gathering, I look at Ernie's painting of us and smile

CHAPTER 7—I DIDN'T KNOW I WAS IRISH UNTIL I WAS FORTY-TEEN

It Helps to Define the Problem

There was a really big group of Loras College seniors in both my class and the class right behind me who went to the University of Iowa Law School in Iowa City. The first half of my freshman year was a mystery. I took every exam and clearly defined what the best answer was to each problem and why that was the case. For a half a year, I got nothing but Cs for test grades. I could not figure out what was going on until one day I went downtown and stopped into a local bar. There I met a half-dozen fellow law students who were veterans of the Korean War. As we were drinking beer, I told them what I was doing and asked them what the problem was. Their answer surprised me. They told me that the professors wanted a list of all possible answers, why they were possible and perhaps what additional information was needed in order to make that possibility a reality. Thank God for Budweiser! After that, law school was not all that hard and I ended up with a Juris Doctor degree. I married Priscilla Dee Brown at the beginning of my last year of law school. The first of our four sons, Harold, was born in Iowa City shortly before I graduated from law school.

My first real legal job was as an Assistant Attorney General from 1965 through 1969 assigned to what was then the Iowa State Highway Commission in Ames, Iowa. Four years later, I joined the Right-of-Way office of the Iowa State Highway Commission that ultimately became the Iowa Department of Transportation. I became its Right of Way Director for Administration and served there for twenty years. When I left the Iowa Attorney General's Office, my brothers Tom and Joe spent a long weekend with me to finish building the lower level of our new house at 345 Rookwood Drive north of Ames. This made it possible for Priscilla's mother, Dorothy Quan, to live with us. It also allowed our four sons, Harold, Daniel, Charles and Matthew, to attend Gilbert grade and high school and to remain members of St. Cecilia Church in Ames.

When we first joined St. Cecilia's, the church was across the street from what was then the Iowa State Highway Commission Headquarters on Lincoln Way in Ames. While our sons Charlie and Matthew were yet to be born, I worked with Bob Walsh, Bill Reese, and Bill Zmolek to create the St. Cecilia's high-school religious education program for the freshman class and taught the program for twenty years. This was a wonderful and creative time for all four boys.

All four boys were Mass servers all through high school and were often called upon to serve for both weddings and funerals. Their grade school and high school years were a wonderful time for us all, except for one time. That time was when Jim Kleinschmidt was crippled and became totally paralyzed while riding his bicycle home from our religious education program. When I told the boys about Dick Kehoe's accident when I was in high school at Loras Academy, they cried. We all prayed for Dick and Jim. We would occasionally visit Jim at his home where his mother cared for him. Jim could not speak, walk, or even sit up in bed. What Jim could do was smile. He did that every time we visited him.

Our four boys and I worked and played together all through their high-school years. I remember a time when Matthew was still in grade school and all four boys helped me to create a great looking yard at our home on Rookwood Drive. The problem one spring was the removal of dandelions. I asked the boys to remove fifty dandelions a day so that none went to seed. Harry, Dan and Charlie showed me their work when I got back from the office. The count was right and I thanked them. Instead of leaving and doing something else, they waited until I took a look at Matthew's bucket of dandelions. I noticed that Matthew's bucket contained dandelions that were all withered up. I asked him if he dug those dandelions today. He looked at me and waited for a few seconds. Finally he said that he had not picked them today. That satisfied the other three boys and Matthew finished his job. It still brings a smile to my face when I think of it.

Family Scale-Model-Airplane Collection

I think the most creative thing we did together was to build our outstanding scale-model-airplane collection. I still have six Graham family trophies for winning area-wide scale-model contests sponsored by the Ames Main Street Modeling Store. I know that Charlie and Harry also took their trophies with them when they grew up. All four boys and I worked in our basement modeling room for ten years. The Graham scale-model-airplane collection consists of 679 model airplanes. The collection's narrative inventory is forty-two pages long.

In order to house the entire collection of built models, we built four, glass-doored, shelved display cabinets (8' x 6' x 2'). The Graham boys learned their own design and creative construction skills. The basic specialty of the entire collection was not just authentic identification and paint schemes. It was also the fact that everything works on the models. They can be displayed with wings and wheels up or down, with cockpit open or closed, and with or without the pilot. Hopefully someday we will find a proper location to safely and properly display the whole collection. The scale models themselves have been carefully packed and preserved in a secure annually inspected airplane trailer. I designed this trailer to hold the World War I, Newport 17, biplane single-seat fighter that I always wanted to build but never had the time to do it.

Family Pheasant Hunting

Every year while we lived at Rookwood Drive, my brothers Tom, Joe, John and I, and our kids, went pheasant hunting around New Hampton, Iowa. Our family was the continuing guests on the farm of Leonard and Terry Franzen. We all hunted together and ate together and had a wonderful weekend. When we began this, Harry and Dan, and then later Charlie and Matthew, were our hunting dogs. We would send the kids into the bushes and rough spots to scare the pheasant out. Sooner or later they too carried a single-shot shotgun. Unlike today, in those times there was a great abundance of beautiful pheasants.

When the day's hunting was over, we would all gather in New Hampton at a local cafe where there was music, dancing and good food. I think it was the year that Harry and Dan were seniors, Charlie was a sophomore and Matthew was in eighth grade. We all had a long, wonderful, and tiring hunting day. We ate dinner at this big cafe in New Hampton where there was a wedding reception in progress. All of our kids joined in with the music and danced with the girls and had a great time.

In the room where everyone was dancing, there was a full-size cardboard cutout of a very beautiful scantily clad girl carrying a tray with glasses of beer. At about eleven o'clock, my brother Tom and I got tired and we went to our room to get some sleep. When I woke up the next day, this scantily clad beautiful girl was in my room. I guess that made sense. If the café owner went looking for it, they knew I left early and would not look in my room. But using the same train of thought, if they knew that our kids stayed late, and if they searched their room, they would not find it because I had it. The last time I saw this scantily clad, beautiful girl was at my son Charlie's Loras College dorm room.

Every hunting year was better than the one before. From a family fun point of view, pheasant hunting was a little piece of heaven. All the cousins got to meet one another and play with one another

147

in a way that was impossible at any other place or time, except for what was to come later at the Graham Frentress Lake cottage family gatherings. I also remember hearing what I thought might be a good hunting song while driving up to New Hampton.

It went like this: *"Heaven's just a sin away, hallelujah, hay, hay, hay."* When I got to New Hampton and we were all gathered together for an evening meal, I told all of the kids about my proposed song. But when I sang the song to them, the kids all had puzzled expressions. I asked them what was wrong. They explained to me that everybody knows that heaven and sin were opposites. I thought about that and concluded that they were right.

In the morning, we stopped at a neighbor's farmhouse and invited the farmer to hunt with us. We all lined up in a cornfield and started walking up the long, gradually rising hill together. The kids started singing the song as we went. While the boys used the basic song when they started singing, they added new words to it. It went like this: *"Heaven's just a sin away, horse shit, hallelujah, hay, hay, hay."* The more I thought about it, adding *horse shit* to the song made it right. The farmer looked at me with a puzzled expression. I shrugged my shoulders and told him: "Who knows where that came from?" Before long, both the farmer and I were singing the same song with the rest of the boys.

When I first realized I was Irish happened about this time during football season. For some reason, all of my life I had watched Notre Dame football. This started when I was in high school and college at 135 South Hill Street in Dubuque. It continued when our family lived at Rookwood Drive north of Ames. I would never miss the Notre Dame and University of Southern California late-night game. It nearly always got so exciting that I went into the kids' bedrooms and woke them up to watch the game. I had told our four boys that their grandfather, my father, Joseph Gill Graham, was Irish and that he had earned a master's degree at Notre Dame. Our family's Irish connection was really made when we started watching these games and jumping up and down at 10:30 at night. A little screaming never hurt anyone!

It's entirely possible that our family's Irish roots might explain some of the fun that our kids and I had in our later efforts to both identify and solve athletic, and professional work problems that were designed and intended by others to have NO solution. The formula is really quite simple. Put it in God's hands. Know your strengths, what is right and give it your all. At the same time, look for and identify the other person's weakness. In rifle team vernacular, once you know his weakness, pull the trigger slowly without a smile on your face. Professional courtesy says that the *least* you should do is wait until no one can see you before you laugh out loud.

CHAPTER 8—GRAHAM FAMILY MOTTO: YES, WE CAN

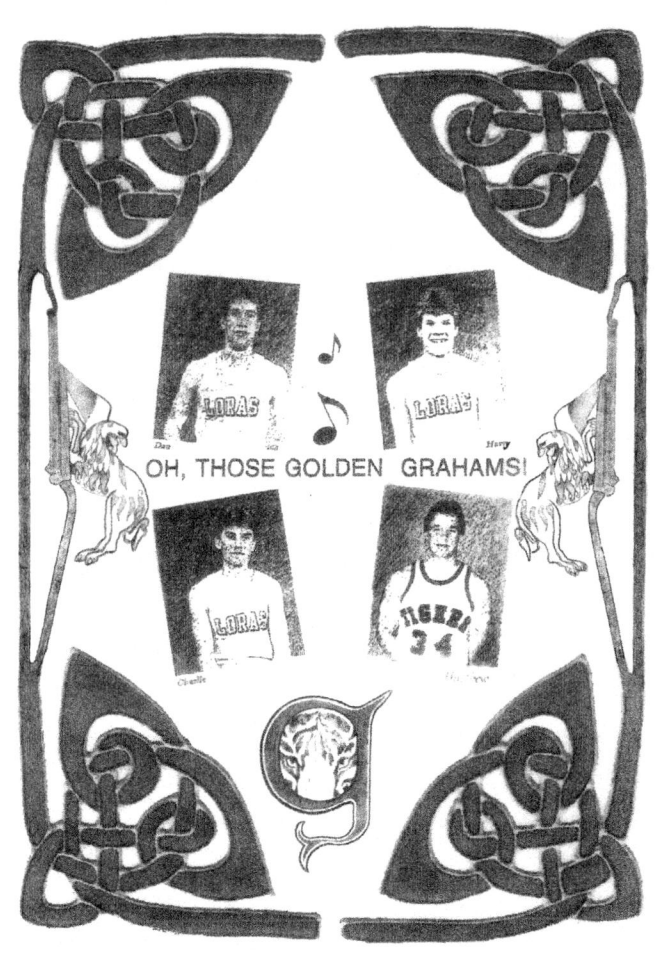

OH, THOSE GOLDEN GRAHAMS!

Harry's Fifth-Grade Teacher's Phone Call Started It All

One day I got a call from Harry's first-grade teacher. She sounded somewhat frantic on the telephone. She said: "Harry's running around in the room. What should I do?" I tried to calm her down. Harry needs to and loves to run. I told her: "Just let him outside to run around the school twice and he will be fine." She did it and everything worked out well. Harry was born to run! When Harry was in grade school, he and his brother Dan were in the same grade. Both of them were among the fastest kids in their class.

In their high-school freshman year, Dan had speed, vision and agility. He could anticipate a tackle or a block and change directions or angles and avoid a disaster. Harry had the speed and endurance but lacked some of the Dan's agility. For a week or so, the seniors and juniors ganged up on Harry. Harry always got blocked. Most of the time, Dan usually avoided being blocked and made the tackle. Then Harry made a mistake.

When the scheduled practice was over, everyone had to run two miles around the track before they could go in and take a shower. Harry passed the juniors and seniors on the run. The upperclassmen would have none of that so they tried to run Harry down. Harry finished well ahead of the rest of the team. Their coach noticed this. The coach made the whole team, except Harry, run two extra laps. By the time the rest of the team finished their extra laps, Harry was coming out of the locker room. He saw two seniors approaching. The seniors were joined by two juniors and they all took off after Harry.

Harry jumped the fence to the adjacent cornfield. He left the upper classmen empty-handed and exhausted in the cornfield. About that time, I pulled into the school parking lot and asked Harry if he wanted a ride home. He told me: "No, thanks, Dad, I think I'll just run home. It's only three miles." Harry was just not made to play football.

In Harry's sophomore year he helped Gilbert's cross-country coach, Ms. Anderson put together a winning cross-country running team. A month after the cross-country season began the new cross-country team won its first trophy Harry took the trophy into the football locker room and told everybody undressing and showering. He told them: "See this? This is a trophy, T-R-O-P-H-Y. Take a good look because you will never see one." He got out the door before anybody could grab him.

As it turned out, all the members of the Gilbert boy's cross-country team were Catholic. Before every meet they would all meet at St. Cecilia's and say a little prayer asking for help to do their best run.

The Race That Boy Scout Pack 157 Could Not Win

Gilbert Boy Scouts provided an opportunity for the Graham boys to learn real leadership skills. This was unlike Gilbert's Cub Scout program where the focus was on learning how to use tools and how to play together as a troop. Racing their hand-carved, pinewood derby wooden race cars was a way to win a trophy and just have fun together. However, being a Boy Scout often represented a real challenge. This was true for each individual Boy Scout who, like Charlie, worked toward and achieved his Eagle Scouting excellence badge. It was also true for the whole scout troop that was challenged to perform campout and athletic contests with other Boy Scout troops.

I remember when I attended the area scout leadership meeting in advance of the two-day spring athletic contests campout. This annual camping trip was a big deal. I came to the meeting informally dressed in order to pick up the schedule of events and the equipment lists we would need. Nearly everyone at the meeting was dressed informally, that is, everyone except, two people who represented an Ames scout troop. These two individuals were in full dress uniform. They kind of controlled the meeting. They also made it clear that their troop expected to again win the trophies for all six of the scheduled events. This all went on for about an hour. Finally, I had an idea. I told the group that we had several new scouts who did not yet have full uniforms and equipment. I was assured that we could compete even though this was the case. To assure our qualifications as a new troop, I received the Gilbert troop's meet flag. I was directed to plant the flag as part of the big circle of tents at the meet.

This was the first competitive opportunity that our Gilbert troop had when I was their troop leader. When I got back to our preparation troop meeting, everybody was gathered around to hear the details of what the meet was going to be all about. I explained all six of the events and what was necessary to win them. Then I told them about the troop that I was told would win all six of the events *again*. I told our scouts that it was explained to me that this troop was a collection of *very superior* and extremely intelligent athletes who were looking forward to another set of guaranteed trophies.

This was intentionally and absolutely the worst thing I could have told our troop. Everyone in the room got really upset. Our meeting was scheduled to be over in an hour. It took two more hours for Harry, Dan, Charlie and the rest of the group to analyze each of the six events and figure out who should be on our team in each event. We had three weeks to get ready for the meet. Every member of our troop ran a mile and a half every day after our meeting, except Sunday.

When it came time for the meet, no one in our entire troop wore the full uniform. This was unlike almost everyone else at the meet. The first day of the meet was a slaughter. In one of the first three events that we ran in, we not only came in first and second, but also third. The second day was not as easy. The other troops were better organized. Gilbert won the first of the three second-day events and then came in second in the second event. The last event, distance swimming, was really close. Harry gave one of the other guys a fighting chance by slowing up a little. He almost slowed up too much and our guys were screaming at him. I don't know what they would have done to Harry if he had not won the race! That evening everybody gathered around the big camp fire so that the trophies could be distributed. Gilbert picked up five of the six trophies, and many of the third, fourth and fifth place ribbons that Charlie and our other younger Boy Scouts earned.

Gilbert High School Track and Cross-Country

Gilbert didn't do much in football when the Graham boys were there, but they really enjoyed and were successful in track with Harry, Dan and Charlie and in cross-country with Harry and Charlie. I remember one time when I was standing at the beginning of the third leg of the two-mile relay at what was then Gilbert High School's brand-new football field and track. Harry ran the second leg of the relay and Dan ran the third leg of the relay. The team to beat that day was Roland Story as they had a seasoned and successful group of distance runners. The race had begun and Harry had just received the baton. Roland Story's runner, McDonald, was talking to Dan and telling him that he did not really know why Gilbert was in the race. He explained how good his team was and felt sorry for Dan because he was about to be humiliated. Dan never said a word until Harry started to get close to his hand off in the lead. Then Dan turned to McDonald, pointed and said: "See this? This is my ass and that is all you are going to see today!" Dan was right. McDonald never got closer than five yards. At the end of this wonderful year, both Harry and Dan accepted a scholarship from Loras College in Dubuque to run on the Loras track and cross-country teams, later to be followed by their brother, Charlie.

When Harry and Dan graduated from Gilbert High School in 1983, the track record board showed:

- 880: Dan Graham

- Mile: Harry Graham

- Two Mile: Dan Graham

- 800 Relay: Dan Graham

- Medley Relay: Dan Graham

- Two-Mile Relay: Harry and Dan Graham

Thirty years later in 2013 I stopped and viewed Gilbert's record board and noticed:

- 1600 Meter: J Hambly, D Wright, D Graham, S Brouse

Charlie graduated from Gilbert High School two years later in 1985. Charlie's class did not have the athletic depth that the class of 1983 had. Charlie's class won track meets and cross-country races by two, three, or five points, not the fifteen or twenty points that the class of '83 did. Even so, the class of 1985 were themselves champions the way they worked so hard together. I remember Charlie's greatest high-school race. It was at the end of the season. The first two runners had times that would clearly qualify for and maybe win at the state meet. Charlie's times were close but not as good as these two runners, but Charlie had a plan.

Two miles is a long distance to run, especially when you're running against some of the best in the state. Neither of the other two runners were concerned with Charlie when Charlie set a very fast pace. Halfway through the race, Charlie was a long distance ahead before the other two runners tried to catch him. When they made their move, I yelled VERY loudly, "CHARLIE!" and Charlie gave it all he had. Halfway through the final lap, Charlie was ahead ten yards. The three of them crossed the finish line not a step apart from one another. The photo finish showed Charlie third by half a step.

One of the greatest honors I have ever received came from Charlie's Gilbert class of 1985 when they invited Charlie and me to give their class commencement address. What a joy-filled time that was!

Son Matthew's Hard but Right Decisions

With his three older brothers all gone to Loras College, Matthew was on his own to help his class be all they could be. Matthew's class was gifted with a lot of good athletes but lacked leadership teammates that Dan and Harry and Charlie's class had. When Charlie left and Matthew was a sophomore, Gilbert had an opportunity to put together a really good football team. This was the time when the United School District dropped football from their curriculum and sent their football players to join the Gilbert High School team. Matthew's class practiced for a week before the United players showed up to join the Gilbert team.

After a week of practice, several Gilbert players expressed concern to the coach that they would never get an opportunity to play once the United players showed up. Gilbert's football coach told the team that he would assuredly play them and that it did not matter to him if the United Community guys were better players. Matthew questioned the coach's meaning and found out that what he had just heard was what the coach promised and intended to do. Matthew told his teammates if that were done it would destroy any opportunity for Gilbert to develop its full potential. Our BEST players need to play if Gilbert was to become a winning football team. At that point, Matthew gave the coach his football helmet and told him that he would no longer be a part of his team. As it turned out, Matthew was right. It was a miserable year for the Gilbert football team that lacked any student leadership.

Matthew was looking forward to track. Unlike his older brothers, Matthew was a powerful sprinter. In his freshman year, he regularly beat juniors and seniors from many schools in the league and was looking forward to his sophomore year in track. When that year came, he was ready and proved it in the first meet with three wonderful sprinting times. In the second meet, however, he strained a leg muscle and lost a month of meet competition time. When you added Matthew to the sprinting skills of three of his other classmates, a state record time was theoretically possible.

Matthew's three brothers all knew this. They knew that Matthew was healthy and came to watch the district meet. Instead of running Gilbert's four best sprinters, the same Gilbert football coach ran Matthew with three, formerly untried freshman runners. Three-quarters of the way through the race, Gilbert's three freshmen were almost fifteen yards behind when Matthew took the baton. When the race was over, Matthew beat two of the five ahead of him and was two steps away from winning the race. His brother Dan timed Matthew's split. We later found out Matthew's split time tied the state record. Matthew never sprinted for Gilbert again.

Basketball was maybe the sport that Matthew enjoyed the most. He always played point guard but was never given the opportunity to play in games in deference to the first team point guard. This remained even though Matthew could and would often out play the first team point guard in practice. At Gilbert's first district state championship qualification game, Gilbert was behind at the end of the first half when Gilbert's point guard got hurt. Matthew had to substitute for him in the second half. By the end of the third quarter, Gilbert was ahead by eight points. Then Matthew was removed from the game. Gilbert lost the game and Matthew never played any more basketball for Gilbert.

After graduation Matthew followed his brothers to Loras College, where, as a sophomore, he played intramural basketball against several teams that included several first team Loras College basketball players. Matthew's team won the Loras intramural basketball championship.

That Christmas vacation, Gilbert had a holiday basketball tournament at the Gilbert gymnasium. Matthew entered a team to play against his old first team. Matthew assembled his neighbors and other players who never received any playing time let alone an opportunity to play in the high-school district tournament. When the game was over, Matthew's second team teammates won the game 49 to the first team score of 25 points.

For the Graham boys, Gilbert High School was a wonderful place for them to grow up. It is no mystery to me that the Graham family motto has always been and will ever be:

YES, WE CAN!

All four Graham brothers attended Loras College in Dubuque. All four of these Graham brothers have done both the Graham family and Loras College proud. The spring 1987 Loras Alumni article was titled: "Oh, Those Golden Grahams!" It was rightfully documented and predictive. As of 2015, four generations of Grahams have graduated from Loras College.

Thank You, Duncan Baird

There is one funny story that needs to be told that took place in the time frame that the four Graham boys were growing up at Gilbert. If my memory is right, Harry and Dan were sophomores in high school and Charlie and Matthew were still in grade school at Gilbert. Duncan Baird worked for me in the Fiscal and Title Section as the condemnation unit supervisor. Duncan put together all of the condemnation application forms with proper legal description, notices and all the other final documents for each and every compensation commission condemnation hearing. When Duncan had questions or issues, he came to me and we worked them out.

Duncan fought all through World War II. He was a multilingual First Sargent in the British Army who served in the Pacific theater. He was a chief noncommissioned officer responsible for the truck equipment training of Indian soldiers. He marched out of Burma to avoid capture by the Japanese and was a British security officer at the Nuremberg war trials after the war.

Duncan and I not only worked together we looked out for one another for twenty years. Duncan had great practical skill and common sense. He had as much unintimidated personal courage as any three people needed. No one could force him to do anything that was wrong or in his mind stupid. For some reason Duncan always liked and helped me. He kept me abreast of what was going on in the right-of-way office. Duncan explained what I was doing and defended me in my effort to restore the highway commission's dysfunctional right-of-way acquisition program. All the while we were together; I never really understood why we liked one another so much. Duncan never married, as his Scottish hometown sweetheart had married someone else while he was overseas in the service.

On one Christmas Eve, I had invited Duncan to have Christmas dinner with us at our home on Rookwood Drive. At this time, the Graham family included my wife Priscilla's mother, Mrs. Dorothy Quan. Mrs. Quan lived in the downstairs apartment that my brothers Tom and Joe helped me build for her fifteen years earlier. While the cooking was going on and the boys were playing downstairs, Duncan and I watched a football game on TV in the living room. We drank a beer or two and philosophizing about life. As Duncan was telling me some of his stories, it was apparent to me that he was unhappy. After another beer I had a solution. I said to Duncan: "Duncan, what you need is the love of a good woman." He responded, "Do you think so, Jimmy?" And of course I answered: "I *do* think so."

What happened next was unpredictable. We all moved into the dining room for Christmas dinner. Duncan was seated right next to Priscilla's mother on the west side of the table. The four boys sat on the opposite east side of the table. I sat on the north and Priscilla sat on the south side next to the kitchen. Duncan took some time and softly told Grandma: "What a BRAW woman you are!" Grandma had a confused expression. She did not know that Duncan had just told her she was beautiful. Duncan talked to Grandma softly. He might have given Grandma the impression that he was thinking about taking her out for a date. Priscilla was speechless and incensed! The four boys tried but failed to maintain blank expressions. They rolled their eyes and looked in different directions, but they kept their mouths shut. It was all that I could do to keep from laughing. To make a long story short, after we finished our meal and Duncan went home, Priscilla banned Duncan from EVER returning to the Graham house.

A little while later, Duncan took some time off and went back to Scotland where he found his old sweetheart whose husband had died. Duncan and his sweetheart, Jeannie, married and they returned to live in Ames, Iowa. While Duncan and Jeannie could not come to our house, I took the four boys to their house for the Halloween Beggar's night and any other excuse I could come up with. I loved both Duncan and Jeannie and I have never had a better friend than Duncan. Duncan finally retired. He and Jeannie moved to Italy and bought a little house in the mountains. I can't remember when, but I heard that he had died. Just because Duncan is no longer with me does not mean that he can no longer help me as you will later see.

CHAPTER 9—ESTABLISHING BASIC ECONOMIC DEVELOPMENT: EMINENT DOMAIN PRINCIPLES

VALIDATED INTERGOVERMENTAL LAND ACQUISITION AGREEMENTS

While the four boys were growing up, my work as an Assistant Attorney General from 1965 to1969 was challenging and creative. Being the youngest member of the staff, I was assigned to do all the matter-of-fact and presumably duller work that the Special Assistant Attorney General did not have time for. This included briefing and arguing Iowa Supreme Court cases that other staff attorneys had lost in the District Court. What I did not realize at the time was that I was ultimately going to spend fifty years as an Iowa Economic Development–Eminent Domain attorney. This Iowa Supreme Court work gave me an opportunity to set permanent administrative and legal standards that would help not only me but also future eminent domain attorneys, engineers, appraisers and realtors not to mention property owners as well.

As the newest and most inexperienced Assistant Attorney General, I was assigned the hopeless work. By definition, this means there was no available persuasive statutory or case law. If there had been such authority the problem would not have existed. This was the work that no one else wanted to do. I had no way of knowing what I was getting into when I received these assignments. It did not take long to figure out why no one else wanted to do the work. In every case the problem was not even clearly defined.

This level of work should have been performed by the Special Assistant Attorney General himself or by his more experienced assistant attorney staff. At the time, I didn't realize what a gift this was to me. I had to keep my promise to my namesake, Father Emmet Kelly, to make the world that I was living in a better place.

The first of these three key Iowa Supreme Court cases was the Garoner v. Charles City a 1966 opinion. In the Garoner case, the City of Charles City had agreed to acquire right-of-way for an Iowa Highway Commission primary highway extension through the city. The landowner's position was, in part, the fact that the project would take his home, which the owner claimed was subject to special statutory protection. I argued and the Supreme Court noted that a 1950 Iowa statute that would deny the city or the Highway Commission the power to take possession of his home without the homeowner's consent had been repealed and was no longer the law. The landowner's position was that he could not replace his home or move all of his personal items and his business property to a replacement site for the purchase price offered by the city.

What I did not realize at the time that I argued this case was how significantly the landowners and businesses were being financially victimized by Iowa's THEN current Economic Development–Eminent Domain system. In 1966, Iowa's eminent domain law forced landowners and tenants to pay their own cost to find and buy or rent comparable replacement housing and the cost to locate and move to a replacement business property. This was the landowner's whole argument in the Garoner case. If this case were tried fifteen years later the landowner would have won the case. This would have been so because the law had changed to require the acquiring authority to provide this relocation assistance and pay moving costs.

After I left the Attorney General's Office and became the Right-of-Way Director—Administration, I participated in drafting nearly all its then current eminent domain and relocation assistance law and implementing policy and procedure. Iowa eminent domain law is found in, Chapter 6A, Eminent Domain Law, Chapter 6B Procedures Under Eminent Domain, and Chapter 316 Relocation of Persons Displaced by Highways.

The fact that Iowa statutory law now provides these property owner rights and benefits does not guarantee that they will actually be provided to landowners. There is now much published case law that demonstrates the consequences of an eminent domain-acquiring authority intentional failure to provide statutorily required property owner rights, benefits and procedural process. The most recent litigated and published case that I am aware of comes from the state of Wisconsin. The case is the City of Janesville v. CC Midwest Inc., 2006 WI App 21. In the City of Janesville case the city was denied a court order or writ of assistance to evict a business from the required property so they could build the project.

The city was denied possession of the property because the city failed to provide a statutorily required comparable business replacement site. The city's position was that there was a site that could be made comparable and that was good enough. The Wisconsin Court of Appeals focused on the specific language of the relocation assistance statute clearly specifying and defining what a statutory comparable replacement business site is. The Wisconsin court denied Janesville the right to take possession of the property to build the project for failure to provide the required replacement business site.

If the 2006 City of Janesville case were tried now in Iowa, the Iowa citizen would have the further protection of Iowa Code Section 6B.57 Procedural compliance. An Iowa landowner could have delayed or prevented the condemnation until the landowner had received all the owner's statutory rights and benefits. See the January 2009 LAD newsletter on the website GrahamLAD.com. It was the absence of current eminent domain landowner rights also found in Iowa Code Chapter 316 Relocation Assistance law that made it impossible for Mr. Garoner to win his 1966 Iowa case.

What the Iowa Garoner case amounted to was only a successful defense of the then standard form of the Iowa Highway Commission's state and local authority joint public improvement intergovernmental agreement process. All Garoner did was to identify the need for the Highway Commission to clarify and standardize its basic intergovernmental project agreement policy and procedure. To accomplish this, I revised and clarified this intergovernmental land acquisition contracting policy and procedure. I then gave this new Highway Commission policy the Iowa Attorney General's approval in my legal opinion indexed as 1970 OAG 92.

ESTABLISHED PROCEDURES TO CLARIFY WHAT PROPERTY RIGHTS ARE ACQUIRED

The most professionally and personally helpful Iowa Supreme Court case that I tried and won as an Assistant Attorney General was Hinrichs v. the Iowa State Highway Commission, a 1967 case. The Hinrichs case involved the construction of interstate Highway

I-80 in Cass County. Mr. Hinrichs asked the Iowa Supreme Court to validate his damage claim caused by the closing of the county road at the interstate highway. He claimed that the value of his farming operation located north of the county road closure was wrongfully decreased because he had to travel farther to get to town. He claimed that he had a contractual right to have the road kept open, noting that he had contributed to the closed county roads' improvement under Iowa Secondary Road code chapter 311.

In the Hinrichs case, the farming operation owned by McCrory and Nelson was divided into both a south farm and the north farm by I-80. The Highway Commission granted Mr. McCrory and Nelson a private right of access to their otherwise physically separated property. This was done by giving them a right to pass *under* the east end of the two interstate bridges. To do so, the landowners agreed to cover any increased cost to redesign the construction of the two bridges over Buck Creek. The landownership title record also needed to be, and was, revised to show their permanent right to use this PRIVATE access route under both bridges.

This created a limited private underpass reconnecting their severed farming operation. Mr. Hinrichs position was that this was an illegal grade separation over the county road because only one person could use it. The Supreme Court noted that no county road adjacent landowner contributing to the snow removal and maintenance of a *county* road acquires a permanent, contractual or ownership right to the closed county road. The court also noted that McCrory and Nelson were not granted use of a *public* highway to the exclusion of any use of the same by Mr. Hinrichs.

The permanent and most useful aspect of the Hinrichs case was that it validated the acquiring authority's right and duty to clearly define what property rights are needed and acquired. The reservation of these private rights to cross underneath the interstate highway bridges was neither fraudulent nor made in bad faith. Nor was it an arbitrary abuse of the highway authority's discretion to reserve or grant these limited property rights to McCrory and Nelson in order to avoid unnecessary damages to their remaining farming operation. The Hinrichs case goes farther. At my request, the Supreme Court also noted that the courts have no power to control the lawful manner in which the highway authority shall exercise the highway design power and authority granted to it by state statute.

I had no idea how useful the Hinrichs case was until I started holding condemnation hearings on behalf of Graham Land Acquisition Associates (GLAA) for city, county and utility clients after I left the Iowa DOT twenty-plus years later. This is clearly and authoritatively the proper way to document how the public improvement project is to be built and what property or land use rights are to be reserved to landowners. It is amazing how much intentional misinformation can be avoided at the condemnation hearings by filing a valid and binding design-related factual statement at the hearing. The filing clarifies what is being acquired by stating what property rights are being left or retained by the landowner. Making such a title record filing is often the only way the compensation commissioners can be informed of and protected when they reject false, factitious or theoretical landowner or landowner's attorney damage claims.

CLARIFIED STANDARDS TO ADMIT LAND SALES AS EVIDENCE OF THE ACQUIRED PROPERTY

The Bellew v. Iowa State Highway Commission 1969 Iowa Supreme Court case remains the clearest statement of the judicial standard to determine what private land sales can be lawfully introduced as affirmative evidence of the after-value of remaining property where only part of a property is acquired for the public improvement project. The Bellew case was also an Interstate I-80 case but was in Dallas County. The landowner owned four adjacent quarter sections of farmland separated one section from another only by county roads. The interstate highway acquired forty acres that divided the property into three physically separated remaining parts.

The District Court condemnation appeal case was tried by the Highway Commission's Special Assistant Attorney General and another Highway Commission senior staff attorney. The case was presented to the District Court judge as opposed to a jury. Over the objection of the Highway Commission's legal counsel, the District Court allowed the landowner's appraiser to wrongfully offer the sale prices of various small tracts of distant small commercial properties as evidence of the value of the Bellew farm. The sale prices of these small properties were not legally admissible as comparable sales evidence of the market value of either the before or the after value of the Bellew farm. The Highway Commission's argument was that the systematic admission of this incompetent land sale evidence was fraudulent where it detracted from and depreciated the weight of properly admitted evidence of other reasonably comparable sales so that the District Court was led into unnecessary confusion.

The District Court's written finding of facts stated that the trial judge did *not* take these distant commercial sales into consideration for purposes of valuing the Bellew farm property. Even if this were true, the District Court's admission of these sales as evidence is in itself a reversible error that should have given the Highway Commission a new trial. The court's finding of facts showed that the judge also wrongfully separately valued the remaining three parts of the plaintiff's farm in arriving at the after-value of the property. This was in direct violation of the requirements of the Iowa eminent domain law requiring that they be valued together or as a remaining unit.

After the trial the District Court judge understood that he had wrongfully admitted this constitutionally prohibited commercial property sales evidence. The judge attempted to avoid a retrial. He did so by simply stating that he did not consider the wrongfully admitted evidence in reaching his value conclusion. In theory this was all that the District Court judge needed to do in order to validate his condemnation award of the difference between the before-taking and after-taking value of the farm.

After the District Court refused to give the Highway Commission a new trial, the Special Assistant Attorney General brought the case file into my office. He threw it on my desk and told me to file an appeal to the Iowa Supreme Court. He told me that this case was total frustration and they didn't have much hope that we would win an appeal. After researching the huge trial record, I found only one time in the three-and-a-half-day District Court trial that the trial court failed to theoretically fix its error in overruling the Highway Commission's objection to the wrongfully admitted sales. He failed to state that he did not consider this one sale in reaching his land value conclusion. This was the one and ONLY time the trial court record did not specifically say that he did not consider the wrongfully admitted evidence. Even though this happened only this one time in the entire record, the Supreme Court noted it and considered it a reversible error.

The other more obvious key to obtaining a new trial was the fact that the District Court used these small distant commercial property sales to wrongfully place separate values on the three physically separate remainder parts of the farm in arriving at the just compensation after-value of the remaining farm. The District Court refused to strike the landowner appraiser's just compensation land value opinions. He did so even though they were based upon this wrongful after-value appraisal method. I also argued that because of this, the trial court did in fact commit an incurable reversible error. The Supreme Court agreed with me.

Aside from winning the case, I had a separate objective in arguing the case. This was to convince the Supreme Court that it was necessary for them to once and for always clearly document what constitutionally required comparable sales evidence admission standards really were. I argued that this problem would never be solved unless these violations automatically resulted in a new trial. To accomplish this, I carefully summarized every Iowa Supreme Court case on these subjects and hoped for the best.

I was not disappointed! The Bellew case helped to effectively put an end to this intentionally incompetent and unpenalized eminent domain appraisal process. The Bellew case was cited in the Iowa Bar Association standard jury instructions for this purpose for years. I had no idea in 1969 how the Bellew case would continue to help me throughout the remainder of my entire Economic Development– Eminent Domain legal career.

What I could not realize at the time the Bellew case was decided was that the Iowa legislature would revise Iowa Code Section 6B.33: Costs and attorney fees in 2006. This code section now requires the acquiring authority to pay the reasonable cost of one appraisal obtained by the landowner in the negotiation process if the condemnation award exceeds 110 percent of the final offer prior to the condemnation. Landowners now may hire their own licensed appraiser and have the appraiser appear and testify at the compensation commission hearing. By law, compensation commissioners are not licensed Iowa attorneys. Thus, compensation commissioners are not responsible to read and apply the land sale evidence standards of the Bellew case. Compensation commissioners cannot and should not be responsible to reject fraudulent landowner professionally prepared appraisals.

Landowners, their legal counsel, and their appraiser now have a new forum or opportunity where they can ignore the requirements of the Bellew case. At this point, there is only one way that the landowner's legal counsel and appraiser can be held accountable for the use of such inadvertent or intentionally incompetent land sale evidence. To do so the acquiring authority must bring it to the attention of the appropriate state legal and appraisal licensing authorities. In order to preserve the future integrity of the system, this is what can and should be done. For this purpose, the Bellew case is just as valuable in 2015 as it was in 1969.

CHAPTER 10—CLARIFED HIGHWAY CONSTRUCTION CONTRACTOR AND LANDOWNER RIGHTS

Construction Contractor Rights

When I became an Assistant Attorney General, the Iowa Supreme Court had struck down the Iowa State Highway Commission's administrative powers to require construction contractors to leave their equipment on the job even though rain, mud and weather made it impossible to work on the project. This was perceived by commission engineers as a major insult to their engineering authority and leadership. As a result of this, Iowa Supreme Court ruling the basic highway construction contract had to be redrafted. The commission had to establish a system that would enable contractors to work on projects in other locations that were not shut down by the weather. I was assigned to redraft the Highway Commission's basic construction contract to enable contractors to do so shortly after I became an Assistant Attorney General.

The Highway Commission's two Division Director engineers, Don McLean and Robert Givens, were assigned to work with me. Neither engineer wanted to be responsible for the loss of ABSOLUTE discretion in the administration of construction contracts. I worked with both engineers for six weeks and accomplished nothing. Then I wrote a letter to the Chief Engineer Howard Gunnerson explaining that it was necessary to remove these two engineers from this construction contract redrafting project and replace them with two other engineers who would listen and cooperate. I had no idea of the level of long-term mistrust and controversy this request would create. Even so, these two senior engineers were given a choice to cooperate and assist or be replaced. They stayed, and we finally got it done.

Paying Landowners on Time

Throughout these first four years as an Assistant Attorney General, I was also working directly with Gordon Sweitzer, the new Right-of-Way Director and retired Marine colonel who was not an engineer. Mr. Sweitzer was hired to straighten out the administrative and procedural mess that the Right-of-Way Office was in. Mr. Sweitzer explained to me in both specific and general terms what needed to be done. He talked me into joining the Right-of-Way Office as its Administrative Director. It ultimately took ten years (1970 through1980) to reorganize and to procedurally document the legal implementation and operation of the entire office. This was to be done by developing Policy and Procedure Manuals for every section of the office and also for both a proposed Condemnation unit and Title and Closing unit of what was to become the new Fiscal and Title Section of the Right-of-Way Office.

The first item on the agenda before we got to writing policy and procedure manuals was to figure out how to pay property owners and to obtain timely transfer of ownership of the land, or easement right to use land, needed to build the project. The objective was to pay property owners and to take possession of the right-of-way for the project in one month after the agreement was signed. The then current landowner payment system often took six months or more. Payment was not made by the right-of-way office that presumably knew what contract obligations were. Instead, payment was made by a combination of one of the six District Offices where the project was located and the Accounting Office. Under the then current system, the Highway Commission took possession of some property for construction purposes before landowners were even paid.

After a study of the system, I recommended changes in the administration of the entire payment system itself. This recommendation would make the right-of-way office responsible for timely and appropriate payment. One missing resource was a licensed realtor *with* legal supervision in the right-of-way office and a small trained staff. This new staff would be responsible to draft payment vouchers and transfer documents in accordance with a legal policy and procedure manual that did not then exist.

This recommendation was drafted and submitted to the Highway Commission Chief Engineer. District engineers were concerned about losing control over the land acquisition payment process. I requested that the proposal be studied. I worked with the newly hired employee assigned to make the study. I pointed out that my proposal would reduce payment errors and staff time in both the accounting and district offices. It would accomplish our goal to provide prompt and proper payment while also assuring receipt of good title and ownership or easement right to use of the land.

When the Chief Engineer's study was completed, it concluded that there was no need to make any change in the payment system. The study report documented the present system. Every engineer that had any Highway Commission administrative responsibility was present when we discussed my proposal and the consultant's report. It took the consultant about a half an hour to explain what he was proposing to do. When it was over I was asked for my comment. I stood up in front of the whole group. I didn't say anything for a minute or maybe two while everyone waited for my reply.

I summarized what they had just heard from the Director's staff person by saying: "What we have just heard are the semilucid ramblings of a bumbling idiot." There was total silence in the room. I waited for another minute. I told the assembled District Engineers that there is an Irish saying that described where this landowner payment process was. It is called Murphy's Law. It goes like this: "Whatever can go wrong will go wrong." I told them that it was just a matter of time before landowners who were not paid their agreed-upon just compensation before construction began would figure out how to stop the project construction until they were paid. When that happened, there would be no one to blame but the District Engineers.

I told them that in my judgment the District Engineers were wrongfully required to practice law without a license. I pointed out that I was a licensed attorney and would set up and supervise the landowner payment and title closing system. I assured them that this new system would pay the right people on time and obtain ownership of all of the right-of-way the Highway Commission needed for the project. I then took each consultant proposal, one at a time, and explained why it would not work. It did not take the District Engineers long to accept my proposal.

I worked with the Iowa Land Title Association and developed the Report of Record Ownership and Liens, still current, landownership report form and system. For the first time, the right-of-way office had all the record title information it needed to both identify and acquire good title to the required right-of-way. A few months after my proposal was approved, I talked right-of-way agent Raymond Callahan into getting his Iowa realtor's license. Ray Callahan became the first Title and Closing Unit Supervisor responsible to pay the right people and to do so on time. For the first time, the Highway Commission landowner title search and payment process actually worked.

Sixty days after my proposal was accepted, the Director's staff person who prepared the report was selling used cars in Mason City. I am informed and hope that my Fiscal and Title Section how-to-do-it policy and procedures manual still exists but in a different format.

Victor the Viper Episode

I think it was shortly before the Iowa State Highway Commission (ISHC) became the Iowa Department of Transportation (IDOT) that the governor hired a new IDOT director by the name of Victor Pricer. Mr. Pricer was hired and directed to create the most cost effective and efficient Highway Commission that was possible. At that time, Gordon Sweitzer and I were both attending the commission meetings. We presented signed contracts for their approval and obtained consent to institute condemnation proceedings where necessary. All these monthly discussions took place in the commission public meeting room, which was attended by the press. At this meeting, Mr. Sweitzer and I were directed by Mr. Pricer to come back with a proposal to cut the Right-of-Way Office operation cost by 10 percent. I told Mr. Pricer that Iowa already was the most efficient right-of-way operation in the Midwest. At that time, I had been working with the International Right-of-Way Association as a chapter and association member, officer, advisor and IRWA course instructor.

This exacerbated Mr. Pricer! He directed me to return next month and document the truth of my assertion. These instructions were, of course, all given in the presence of the press. Being Irish, I got to thinking about how much fun it was going to be for me to give copies of my report to the press. It took ten years to reorganize the Right-of-Way Office so that it implemented legally required project development process and provided statutorily required landowner assistance, payments and benefits. As a byproduct of this effort, every section and subsection of the office operated under written professional subject specific procedural manuals. Every section had access to the policy and procedural manuals of every other section. Questions and issues rarely came up and when they did they were quickly resolved, usually by compliance with the new Right-of-Way Office Administrative Manual.

It took a week for me to simplify and formulate basic generic work accomplishment standards necessary to document right-of-way organizational efficiency. I sent it to the closest thirteen states along with a request that they respond in a timely way. When we received the reports, they documented what we already knew. The Iowa's Right-of-Way operation was, in fact, the most efficient in the Midwest. My perceived personal ethics required that I send the report to Mr. Pricer before the next commission meeting. It was an understatement to say that I was looking forward to a discussion of it. The subject never came up at the meeting. Mr. Pricer stayed as the Commission Director for a while. It wasn't long, however, before he was working for a packing company in Omaha, Nebraska. Soon thereafter, I am told, he was selling used cars in Sioux City.

The National Uniform Act Legislative-Bill-Drafting Fiasco

This episode documents and helps to explain where the Iowa Highway Commission was when I first came to it from the Attorney General's office. It also helps to explain where the Iowa Department of Transportation is at this very moment. This started at the beginning of the federal government's passage of national uniformly required land acquisition and relocation assistance legislation.

This federal legislation applied to every city, every county and all other government authorities acquiring land for any federally funded public improvement purpose. Everyone in the Right-of-Way Office knew that the Iowa Department of Transportation was federally required and responsible to draft the state legislation, implementing administrative rules and also to administer the law. This subject came up at a general IDOT monthly management meeting chaired by Chief Engineer Robert Humphrey.

Mr. Humphrey directed me to draft a legislative bill that would take care of the IDOT's interests only. He told me that cities and counties could do the same to protect their interests. I informed Mr. Humphrey that the federal law required the state's Department of Transportation to prepare the legislation so as to create a uniform statewide system. Then followed a five-minute rant and explicit direction for me to do what I was told. Because I knew, and he needed to know that it was coming, I informed Mr. Humphrey that he would likely soon get a letter from Iowa's governor directing the IDOT to draft the legislation for all Iowa acquiring authorities. Mr. Humphrey opened up his mouth but nothing came out. That was probably a good thing. There were women in the crowd as well. I was obligated too and tried to help him. He was not smart enough to know it.

At our next staff meeting, Mr. Humphrey had actually received the letter from the governor. At the meeting, his face got red, and he talked loud and fast. I thought he was going to blow his cork. It did not do any good that the IDOT's Special Assistant Attorney General confirmed what the IDOT's legislative bill drafting responsibility was. I was informed by Mr. Humphrey that it was my job as an Assistant Right-of-Way Director to do what I was told. He told me that if he wanted to know what the law required he would ask me. To make a long story short, I coordinated and participated in drafting the federally required legislative bill and two implementations of the Iowa Administrative Rules. A few years after Gordon Sweitzer's retirement as Right-of-Way Director, an IDOT Division Director-engineer appointed Robert North, a Right-of-Way Agent who was the Condemnation Unit Hearing Officer and an Iowa-licensed realtor, as the new Right-of-Way Director.

At this time, the Right-of-Way Office was also suffering a continuing loss of all of its experienced and skilled section supervisors, right-of-way acquisition and relocation assistance agents, appraisers and property managers. The new Right-of-Way Director had neither a legal license nor the professional experience necessary to either propose or maintain Iowa's statutorily required land acquisition administrative rules and implementing policy. The required landowner policy and procedural manual protection system responsibility was simply ignored. It was apparent to me what was going to happen. There was no professional future for me in the IDOT Right-of-Way Office. Shortly thereafter in 1990, I left the IDOT and set up my own land acquisition organization, Graham Land Acquisition Associates (GLAA).

One, but not the only, clear and convincing proof of this was that two years after I left the IDOT Right-of-Way Office, my multidisciplined new firm negotiated the purchase of more right-of-way as a consultant for the IDOT than the IDOT bought that whole year with the entire IDOT Right-of-Way Office.

Jim and Jane Marriage

This was a very creative time in my professional life but it was also a very tumultuous time in my personal life. My son Charlie was the last of my four sons to marry when he married in August 1995. Shortly thereafter, my wife, Priscilla, and I separated and our divorce was final in December 1995. I met Jane Ann Pope and her mother Betty Jane Pope while attending Mass at St. Cecilia's Church in October of 1995. I told Jane of my divorce-pending circumstances. She listened to me, didn't say much and told me to contact her when everything was final. Once everything was final, we spent a lot of time sharing our family heritages, work histories, getting to know one another and enjoying the cooking of her mother, Betty.

There was one magic night when everything came together. We went to Hickory Grove Lake southeast of Nevada early one evening. There was no cloud in the sky and the moonlight was nearly as bright as day. When we got to the south side of the lake we parked near the park building and walked to the lake's edge. What we did not realize was that the county was working on rebuilding the lake dam. The lake's water level was down six or eight feet from what was normal. We walked down the bank to the edge of the water to a downed tree on dry land right next to the water that we sat on.

This was the most beautiful nature scene I have ever witnessed. The water was smooth as glass. Both the stars and the moon were reflected in the water from one side of the lake to the other. We must have sat on that fallen tree for ten minutes without saying a word just soaking up the beauty of it all. As we sat there, a muskrat started swimming slowly from west to east right in front of us three feet from the shore The muskrat did not see us and we watched it go by on its way east until out of sight. There was no activity on the north or opposite side of the lake where the swimming beach and the park buildings were. Everything was totally golden bright and quiet. We were the only people on the lake.

As we sat there just soaking in the beauty of it all, we held hands. I asked Janie if she had ever seen anything as beautiful as this. I wondered if we would ever see such beauty again. Janie's response took me totally by surprise. She told me: "Jimmy, what you need is the love of a good woman." I could not believe what I was hearing! Those were the exact same words that I told Duncan Baird while he was sitting next to me in the living room at Rookwood Drive years earlier. I told Janie my Duncan Baird story.

Much to my surprise, she had a Duncan Baird story to tell me. As it turned out, unknown to me, Janie was working in the Right-of-Way Office in 1971 for Duncan Baird. She typed condemnation legal descriptions for him. Janie told me that, three weeks before Janie's daughter Wendi was born, she gave Duncan her notice to quit work. Duncan had asked: "What do you want to take off so early for? Why, my mother had my baby brother Jimmy and was back working in the field in an hour!"

I took Jane's statement about me needing the love of a good woman as Duncan talking directly to me. At that moment, on Duncan's advice, I asked Janie if she would marry me. She said yes! I have thanked Duncan ever since and often tell him in prayer that I owe him a favor.

Jane and I were civilly married in February 1996. The church had completed their review of my application that my first marriage be annulled and formerly approved my request in April 1998. On June 18, 1999, Jane and I celebrated our formal church wedding with my three brothers' families and my four sons, with the exception of my son Matthew and his wife, Sharon, who were in Germany. We were married in St. Patrick's Church at the Irish settlement in Cummings, Iowa. My brother Tom was my best man. Jane's mother, Betty Pope, gave Jane away. Jane's daughter Wendi Fellner served as maid of honor, and she was accompanied by her husband, Peter Fellner.

This was a most fitting place to celebrate our wedding as Jane's maternal ancestral family originated from the Irish settlement and St. Patrick's Church. St. Patrick's Church was first established in 1856. Many Kings and Dooleys were married and are buried at St. Patrick's.

Betty's mother, Teresa, was a King who married Lester Bishop at St. Patrick's Church. Betty was the daughter of Lester Bishop who then married Lester Pope. The *Des Moines Register* newspaper picked this up and published the story. Janie's mother, Betty, brings a smile to everyone's face when she tells this King, Bishop, and Pope family names story.

This all happened when I was in the process of setting up and training the multidisciplinary staff necessary to implement my new public improvement land acquisition organization, Graham Land Acquisition Associates.

It took me until 2000 before I finally figured out why Duncan Baird and I loved and always helped one another as if we were brothers. That was the year that my youngest son, Matthew James, and his wife, Sharon, visited Scotland on vacation. Matthew and Sharon found out that the Graham Scottish and Irish family heritage went back to 1124. Matthew brought back pictures of the Graham castle itself with its huge castle grounds, wall and beautiful formal iron castle entrance gate. This is where the Sixth Duke of Montrose, James Graham, and his wife, Mary Louise, daughter of the Twelfth Duke of Hamilton, lived and died. My wife, Jane, assembled all of Matthew's Scotland castle pictures in a beautiful descriptive oil painting and sent copies to all four of my sons.

When I saw Matthew's information and started to read some Graham family Scottish and Irish history, I finally understood why Scotsman Duncan Baird and I always saw one another as brothers.

Governor-Demanded IDOT Condemnation Study

After I left the Right of Way Office in 1990, the IDOT's right-of-way office began an ongoing decline in the competent administration of Iowa's uniform eminent domain land acquisition system. This continuing lack of competence first became VISIBLE TO THE

PUBLIC in 1997 when Iowa's governor demanded the first-ever official, formal study of IDOT condemnation policy and procedure. This was in response to multiple statewide claims of gross unfairness and incompetence in the IDOT condemnation process. Applying Murphy's Law one would say: "What could go wrong did go wrong!"

I was requested, and agreed to serve on this September 25, 1997, governor's condemnation-process study committee. The purpose of the study was to determine the root causes of alleged premature, inappropriate and illegal condemnation processes. The complaint alleged that there was a state-wide failure in the administration of the right-of-way office condemnation process dating from 1990 when I left the right-of-way office to 1997. The study committee included the Right-of-Way Supervisor for the Federal Highway Administration, John Baty from the Special Assistant Attorney General's Office, three members from the Right-of-Way Office, and me as the President of Graham Land Acquisition Associates. All committee members *initially* agreed to write a unified report to be signed by all members.

All research and report drafting work focused entirely on statistically reporting the appraised amount, the offer made to the landowner and the condemnation award. The committee report was to make no mention of late IDOT appraisals, offers made without an appraisal or for less than the appraised value, failure to consider landowner appraised value information, and both new land sales. and offers of settlement. After I realized this, I informed the committee that, if it was necessary, it was my intention to write a full minority report that would identify all organizational-failure root causes. They believed me, as well they should have. The final committee report identified a total lack of office-wide professional skill and leadership, multisectional mismanagement and office-wide professional leadership incompetence.

The finished final report was lost by the IDOT for months. When the report finally resurfaced, it was sent to the Governor. The Right-of-Way Director was reassigned to a non-right-of-way job until he could retire a year or so later. The IDOT staff engineer who appointed and supervised the Right-of-Way Director also suffered no consequences for this total system failure that I know of. He also retired a few years later.

Governor-Demanded IDOT Appraisal Study

Shortly thereafter in 2003, a group of Iowa-licensed commercial appraisers talked the Governor into requiring the IDOT to hold an Iowa State University–led study of the eminent domain appraisal process. Licensed Iowa commercial appraisers took the position that both the IDOT appraisal manual and their appraisal process ignored nationwide appraisal standards and requirements in the preparation of IDOT eminent domain real estate appraisals.

Several years earlier I had worked with the Iowa Appraisal Licensing Board and had drafted Iowa appraisal licensing legislative changes in the appraisal licensing statute. This appraisal licensing statute now indirectly notifies appraisers of both the nationally required eminent domain appraisal standards and of Iowa's constitutionally required eminent domain appraisal requirements.

These Iowa commercial appraisers told the Governor that the IDOT was ignoring nationwide COMMERCIAL realestate appraisal standards and requirements in the preparation of eminent domain real estate appraisals, which, of course, was true. The workshop had seventeen participants. Five committee members were Right-of-Way office staff. Ten were private appraisers. I was one of two eminent domain attorneys. This whole effort took several months before the private appraisers realized that the IDOT appraisal process was in fact fully compliant with all state and federal legal and administrative requirements. The workshop members determined, issue after issue, that the IDOT appraisal process was also compliant with all constitutionally and statutorily required eminent domain appraisal standards.

The problem with the IDOT appraisal manual was that before I left the right-of-way office to set up my own land acquisition organization I had no opportunity to add reference to the Iowa case law standards to help explain and validate the IDOT appraisal manual text. These standards documented why the Eminent Domain appraisal process is required to be fundamentally different than for a commercial appraisal. In order to clarify and resolve this for all IDOT real estate appraisers, James T. Hayes Jr., who was then Iowa's most informed eminent domain appraiser, and I team taught Volume 8 Appraising Partial Acquisitions of my ten-volume Land Acquisition Design courses to the entire IDOT appraisal staff. Volume 8 identified and explained Iowa statutory and case law requirements for the benefit of all licensed Iowa appraisers preparing an eminent domain appraisal. These Volume 8 case law summaries and legal standards were first made a part of the IDOT Right-of-Way Office Appraisal Operational Manual in 2003.

The IDOT Local Public Agency Manual Study Subversion

There was a time in 2006 when it was still possible for the IDOT Right-of-Way Office to conduct an informal internal review of their operating procedures to determine if they were appropriate and legal. This was under the direction of a then broadly experienced new Right-of-Way Director engineer, Ronald Otto. My continuing experience with Mr. Otto was tied to Iowa projects where Graham Land Acquisition Associates was acquiring right-of-way for cities, counties and utilities on local public improvement projects.

IDOT Right-of-Way Office Local Public Agency (LPA) staff was constantly demanding that my city, county and other clients implement legal and administrative requirements in an improper, uninformed and often illegal manner. From 1990 to 2007, I tried to help the IDOT Right-of-Way Office Director to recognize his staff's failure to implement required landowner procedural protections and to provide required landowner and tenant benefits and services. This is fully documented in *Volume 10—Managing Land Acquisition Organizations*. The complete text for Volume 10 is set out in the website: GrahamLAD.com. After four or five years of me correcting the IDOT Right-of-Way Office Local Public Agency (LPA) staff as necessary to protect my clients and landowners, Mr. Otto determined that it was necessary to substantively review both the *IDOT Right-of-Way Office Administrative Rules* and their *Local Public Agency Policy and Procedural Manual*.

This was six years prior to the more recent statewide, much publicized, right-of-way property management staff systematic long-term theft of IDOT excess land property management income with its criminal charges and consequences. The first article on this subject claiming the IDOT's loss of $240,000 was publicized in Iowa's *Des Moines Register* paper April 21, 2013.

This state and local government committee for the study of a proposed Right-of-Way Office (LPA) manual included five city staff, one county engineer, one private professional engineer, three IDOT right-of-way appraisal staff and myself. What the committee's city, county and professional members did not realize until near the end of the study itself was that the entire study was a sham. While the committee would be discussing policy and procedural manual drafts, the IDOT was filing changes to the Iowa Administrative Rules. These administrative rule changes further reduced statutorily required landowner procedural rights. The committee knew nothing of what the IDOT was doing to revise the Iowa Administrative Rules and had no opportunity to comment on it.

The Attorney General's office had previously provided Mr. Otto with an informal unpublished legal opinion that Iowa's statutorily law required a ninety-day notice and that it had to be given to landowners at the *end* of negotiations after an agreement was signed or a condemnation award had been paid not on the day that negotiations *began*. Mr. Otto provided me with a copy of this informal Attorney General's legal opinion for my information in connection with an earlier GLAA project before he decided to put this committee together. Before the committee could meet and discuss the legality of this and several other IDOT existing policy and procedural requirements, Mr. Otto had a heart attack and was not available to manage the committee.

The study committee members found out, near the end of the study of the Local Public Agency Manual, that the Right-of-Way Office had already submitted proposed Iowa Administrative Rules that would require the ninety-day notice to landowners to be given on the very day of the first negotiation contact. That information and the factual or procedural need or legal reason for it was never provided to the committee. Under Iowa law, the acquiring authority has no right to take possession of property needed for a public improvement any sooner than when the landowner agrees to give possession or after the acquiring authority has deposited the condemnation award with the sheriff. This 90-day notice administrative rule totally failed to provide the landowner the possessory benefit intended by the Iowa statute. As written, this notice rule also undermines good faith negotiation where the rule falsely implies acquiring authority possessory rights that do not exist.

To my knowledge no formal Attorney General or any other legal opinion was ever requested by the committee chairman. No legal opinion was ever provided to the committee on any subject that was questioned or discussed in committee meetings. Neither did the Special Assistant Attorney General nor any attorney on its staff ever participate in or, to my knowledge, ever provide any information to anyone that was ever shared with the committee.

Instead, the committee's effort was directed solely to a review of both the November 15, 2006, IDOT draft public and the new *private* internal (LPA) manual. Committee meetings also proceeded without obtaining any legal review or discussion of the appropriateness or legality of any of the several identified and questioned draft manual procedural requirements or issues. As a result, *very* soon nearly all city and county committee members stopped coming to committee meetings. IDOT committee members ended up talking to themselves. It was over!

What is needed to procedurally fix Iowa's current dysfunctional economic development–eminent domain land-acquisition regulatory and administrative system is fully set out in my December 18, 2006, letter to the then new Right-of-Way Director Martin Sankey. This letter was in response to Mr. Sankey's request for comments on the then new draft Right-of-Way Office Local Public Agency (LPA) manual. The six factual observations in this letter fully and completely describe why and how the current IDOT right-of-way process is an intentional violation of Iowa acquiring authority powers and duties. The letter also makes five specific recommendations on how to fix this intentionally dysfunctional IDOT Local Public Agency (LPA) system. Nothing has changed since 2006. As a matter of professional courtesy the December 18, 2006, letter to Mr. Sankey was not published. It is available to anyone who wants it.

The proper coordination of the multiprofessional skill and experience needed to do the right-of-way acquisition job right the first time was the reason for me writing the first nine of my Land Acquisition Design (LAD) courses. This LAD course development all happened after I left the Right-of-Way Office of the Iowa Department of Transportation in 1990 and set up Graham Land Acquisition Associates. There really is no administrative fix for Iowa's broken system. The reasons for this are documented in the May, June, July and August 2013 LAD Newsletter and the December 2014 LAD newsletter both of which are available in their entirety on the website: GrahamLAD.com.

International Right-of-Way Association (IRWA) courses are all non-state specific training programs. For this reason, no IRWA course can be applied directly to identify, implement or maintain Iowa's specific constitutional and statutory legal eminent domain requirements. I say this as a person who was a member of Iowa Chapter 41 of the International Right-of-Way Association for twenty years. I became a Certified Instructor for IRWA and began teaching their courses in 1976. I still have a plaque given to me in 1981 in Recognition of Outstanding Service as President of Chapter 41. The Right-of-Way Professional of the Year award was also given to me by the International Right-of-Way Association in 1985 in Recognition of Long and Meritorious Service to Iowa—Nebraska Chapter 41. The

1985 plaque was given in part to recognize my assistance in helping the Association draft their generic multiprofessional training courses.

Now, every Iowa acquiring authority has to figure out for itself how to comply with the IDOT Local Public Agency policy and procedural manuals. Cities and counties also have to figure out how to provide contradictory legally required land acquisition and relocation assistance notices, payments, benefits, and information mandated by Iowa statutory law. As of 2015, the only place and way that these statutory legal requirements and issues can be systematically identified by cities, counties and utilities is for them to read both the monthly *Land Acquisition Design* Newsletters and *Volume 10 Managing Land Acquisition Organizations* all of which are available on the website GrahamLAD.com.

Here we are again back in 1965, except that this time it is not the District Engineers who are practicing law without a license. Now it is the Right-of-Way Office itself that is practicing law without a license. It is doing so where it fails to both recognize and to provide landowners their substantive and procedural assistance, rights, benefits and payments as required by both federal and state law and regulation. Common sense and observation tells me that since I left the right-of-way office in 1991 Murphy's Law was working overtime to create the present dysfunctional system. Those responsible for its failure, sooner or later may, or may not, receive proper credit for doing so. In the meantime, it is the landowners and Iowa's city, county and other eminent domain acquiring authorities that are suffering the consequences of Iowa's broken system.

Iowa Eminent Domain System Is Fixable If You Know How and Why It Is Broken

I think it was in my first or second year as Right-of-Way Director for Administration of what was then the Iowa Highway Commission that the question of buying more land than what was needed for a public improvement project first came up. The Highway Commission could not negotiate the purchase of right-of-way required to build and maintain the highway for the diagonal segment of Interstate I-35 north of Ames.

The reason for this was that condemning only the needed right-of-way would leave existing farming operations separated by the highway and otherwise in shambles. Some farmers would have miles to drive in order to farm isolated and irregular-shaped remaining pieces of the original farm.

At this time, the Iowa Code Section 306A.5 Acquisition of property and property rights was passed. This new power enabled the Highway Commission to acquire triangular or strip uneconomic remnant remaining farmland through a negotiated purchase or by condemnation where the interests of the public would be best served even though all the land was not needed for the right-of-way proper. This law empowered the IDOT to purchase uneconomic remnants. It also helped landowners to relocate from their damaged farming operations on the diagonal Interstate I-35 north of Ames.

The management of acquired triangular and other unneeded farming remnants was provided by the Right-of-Way Office under my direction. These remnants were rented and resold in the real estate market after the construction of the project. For twenty years, this was done very ethically, profitably and transparently by Erling Larson, the Right-of-Way Office Property Management Section Supervisor before his retirement a year or so after I left the office in 1990.

More recently, for good and just reasons, the Iowa Code Section 6A.21 Condemnation of agricultural-land definition now specifically forbids the purchase of agricultural land for PRIVATE DEVELOPMENT purposes. A public use or public purpose is defined to exclude acquisitions for private development purposes *unless* the owner of the agricultural land consents to the condemnation. Iowa Code Section 6A.22 Additional limitations on exercise of power—definitions also forbids the condemnation of private property for private use incidental to the public use of property or solely for the purposes of facilitating incidental private use.

The basic standard to determine what additional land not needed for the project could be involuntarily acquired by condemnation is generally set out in Iowa Code section 6B.3 Application recording notice time for appraisement new proceedings, subsection g. Before the acquiring authority can obtain title or ownership, as opposed to a temporary easement right to use the property for the construction and maintenance of the public improvement, there must be a showing that a substantial PERMANENT NEED exists for the additional property to achieve the public use or purpose (or) that the land constitutes an uneconomical remnant that has little or no value or utility TO THE OWNER (or) lastly where the owner CONSENTS to the condemnation.

For a full explanation and illustration of how this should but clearly does not always work to protect the landowner, see the September 2013 and the February, March and April 2014 LAND ACQUISITION DESIGN newsletters on GrahamLAD.com.

There is at least one other basic project financing factor that helps to explain ongoing failures to inform and provide landowners their statutory procedural rights. In part this goes back to Iowa's Constitution. Consider that the eminent domain paragraph of Article 1 section 18 of the Iowa's Constitution empowers the IDOT, cities and other Iowa eminent domain authorities to acquire farmland and other property for its present value *without* taking into consideration any land value or other advantages that may result to the owner on account of the improvement for which it is taken. This is the definition of the eminent domain appraisal standard required by the Iowa Constitution.

For example, the condemnation of a landowner's property not needed to construct and maintain a commercial highway interchange deprives the landowner of an opportunity to sell the owner's remaining property for its new higher and more valuable use. Alternatively, the condemnation of *excess* land or land not needed for the public improvement project in cities and development areas enables the IDOT or other acquiring authority to help fund the cost of the public improvement project itself. It does so by selling the property *after* the completion of the project for its new *after*-project completion *much* higher land value. It does so at an indirect and wrongful loss to the property owner who no longer owns the unneeded excess land.

The most factually egregious illustration of Iowa acquiring authorities apparently intentional ignoring statutory property owner rights and statutory acquisition limitations that I am aware of is the subject of the February, March, April 2014 LAD newsletter on GrahamLAD.com. The added benefit of this 2014 LAD newsletter is that it also identifies the need to make statutory clarification to Iowa Code Section 6B.52: Renegotiation of damages. Landowner's need this five-year statutory right to clearly *require* acquiring authorities to renegotiate damages for the wrongful acquisition of property not needed for the public improvement project.

Language for a draft legislative bill proposal to give landowners the RIGHT to renegotiate an acquiring authority's wrongful acquisition or condemnation of excess land or land not needed for the construction and maintenance of the project is also included in this February, March, April 2014 LAD newsletter. Acquiring authorities can avoid any problem by identifying unneeded land as *excess* land and obtaining the landowner's consent to purchase or condemn it. Acquiring authority failure to do so *should* enable the landowner to renegotiate the acquisition and to obtain return of title and ownership as unforeseen damages.

I have often been asked, and have asked myself, what are the chances that Iowa's Economic Development–Eminent Domain system will ever be fixed to properly inform and protect landowners? The federal law requires state DOT's to implement a national uniform public improvement land acquisition system. This system provides landowners with specified procedural and substantive land acquisition and relocation assistance property owner rights and benefits. This is in addition to, but MUST ALSO INCLUDE, notice of State of Iowa property owner rights, which are separately required by state statute. Good faith negotiations require the acquiring authority to provide property owners with a written statement of *all* of their individual rights and basic protections under Iowa eminent domain and relocation assistance law.

The May 2009 LAD newsletter and attachments details and identifies all property owner statutory and regulatory rights. The present IDOT landowner information system picks and chooses what legal rights they will recognize and directly inform landowners of. At the present time no landowner will ever know what his or her rights are without hiring an eminent domain experienced attorney.

This is neither just nor reasonable. It is not the way the Economic Development–Eminent Domain system is intended to and needs to work. How to do the job the right way is the subject of the first nine LAD courses and the LAD 2008–2014 monthly newsletters. The May 2009 LAD newsletter documents rights, payments and benefits many of which are no longer identified, or provided by the IDOT Right-of-Way Office, with or without the advice of the Attorney General's office.

Where Iowa's Economic Development–Eminent Domain system is now and why it is intentionally broken is fully set out in the December 2014 LAD newsletter available in its entirety in GrahamLAD.com. Note the February 10, 2014, MEMORANDUM to the Iowa Bar Association Government Practice Section March 28, 2014, seminar attendees. This memo reports on an IDOT Right-of-Way Office and Federal Highway Administration (FHWA) sponsored two-day seminar taught by IDOT Right-of-Way staff. I attended the program along with fifty other city, county, and utility public improvement land acquisition staff.

IDOT Right-of-Way Office Local Public Agency presenters wrongfully informed us that the landowner moving costs payments under Iowa Code Section 6B.44 Taking property for highway—buildings and fences moved is a taxable payment for federal income tax purposes. Similarly they wrongfully advised us to tell landowners that moving costs paid as relocation assistance payments under Iowa Code Section 316 Relocation of persons displaced by highways had to be considered as taxable severance damages for income tax purposes. The stated purpose for telling landowners this is to avoid the acquiring authority responsibility to move and/or pay for both of these statutorily required moving expenses.

The May, June, July and August 2013 LAD newsletter transmits the entire text of *Volume 10 Managing Land Acquisition Organizations* as an integral part of the Graham LAD.com website itself. Volume 10, in turn, provides a complete factual history of the author's thirty-year, unending effort to protect his Graham Land Acquisition Associates (GLAA) Iowa acquiring authority clients and landowners themselves from the identified ongoing maladministration of Iowa's economic development–eminent domain system.

The fix is simple! The Iowa code needs to require that the IDOT Right-of-Way Office Director be a licensed Iowa attorney. The Attorney General's office must also be required by law to assist the

IDOT in the development of required land acquisition administrative rule and implementing administrative policy and procedure. As of January 2016, the Iowa Department of Transportation, the Iowa Bar Association and the Iowa Attorney General's offices do not acknowledge the problem. What are the chances that this will ever be fixed? YES, WE CAN!

CHAPTER 11—IT IS GOOD TO ENJOY YOUR WORK

This chapter of *South Hill Rascals* focuses on the professional challenge, fun and satisfaction that licensed professionals can have by doing the job the right way. Each of these four episodes starts with the factual summary of what the project was all about. At that point, put yourself into the picture as you read what happened and how it all unfolded. This is the work that I was brought into this world to do.

Right-of-way acquisition work for public improvement projects is a multiprofessional challenge. It is also fun and very much interprofessionally satisfying when it is done right. The only projects that are successful are those that effectively coordinate the work of all state licensed professionals. These licensed professionals include land surveyors, engineers, real estate appraisers, realtors as acquisition negotiation and relocation assistance agents, eminent domain attorneys and last but not least real estate property managers.

These four public improvement projects illustrate some typical project development complexities. More importantly, they provide insight into the *real* joy and satisfaction there is in doing this interdisciplinary professional work the right way. When you get to the end of the factual summary of each episode you will have become part of the story itself. Ask yourself what you would have done? Maybe even better, ask yourself if you would have laughed or maybe even celebrated it? Believe me: I DID, or maybe I should say, WE did!

CITY OF TAMA — FLOOD CONTROL PROJECT

Soon after I left the Iowa Department of Transportation and established Graham Land Acquisition Associates in 1990, the

City of Tama asked me to meet with them and officials from the US Corps of Engineers out of Davenport, Iowa. The purpose of the meeting was to determine whether it was possible for the city to make timely acquisition of the right-of-way necessary to construct flood control dikes needed to protect the city from reoccurring floods. So much time had been spent in the engineering design phase of the project that there was a risk that funding would be lost if right-of-way could not be immediately acquired. The Director of the Davenport office of the US Corps of Engineers advised me to give it up. He told me that all the right-of-way had to be acquired in six months and there were nine condemnations required.

Prior to our meeting with the Director of the Corps of Engineers, my staff and I reviewed all of the landowner parcel files. We had a good idea how difficult the project was likely to be. After I accepted the project, it took us a week just to make a final offer to settle and acquire the properties. We needed that before we could begin condemnation document preparation and filing with the Chief Judge of the Judicial District to even start the condemnation hearing process. To accomplish this, we set up a condemnation document factory producing all documents necessary to obtain condemnation powers and to hold the hearings. When we finished documents for the first parcel, or property, we immediately started documents for the second parcel, then the third, etc.

The Justin Whitzel Story
The Justin Whitzel story was a perfect illustration of what was to come. Mr. Whitzel was an old farmer who operated his farm in the floodplain. When he showed up at the hearing he had his dirty boots on and was wearing an old pair of blue jeans. You could

tell they were an old pair because the right rear pocket of his blue jeans had a big hole in it. This explained why he carried his wallet in the left rear pocket of his pants. Justin carried a wooden cane that looked like he had cut it out from the woods behind his house. Justin brought two attorneys with him. The first attorney was a little younger. He gave the impression that he was the technician or fact finder for the property owner.

The second attorney wore a black suit. It wasn't his suit that looked so impressive; it was his vest and all of the sparkly things that hung from it. He was the leader! That was made clear as he slowly walked around the room sizing everyone up and not saying a word. They had another person with them that I knew to be the recently retired city engineer for the City of Ames that I had worked with on Ames public improvement projects.

When we viewed the property, the city's engineer for the project showed everyone the survey stakes locating where the flood control dam, or berm, was to be built. The engineer asked if there were any questions. After the project's what, why and how questions were answered, we returned to the courthouse. The commissioners had butted two tables end-to-end so that the commissioners all sat in a row with the tables in front of them. I asked our appraiser to explain how he arrived at his opinion of value and the land sales information he used in doing so. I thought he did a good job. I did not think that money would be that big of an issue. All of the nearby, recent farmland sales that he used to arrive at his opinion of land value were located close by and were only a few months old.

Then came one of the good parts. The trial attorney rose to his feet and started walking up and down in front of the commissioner's tables with a concerned expression on his face. His argument was that his client's only opportunity to be justly compensated was TODAY. If the project failed or he suffered unanticipated damage he would never be compensated for it if they did not include it in this award on this day. I could not believe my ears! This went on for a couple of minutes. Before he finished his impassioned plea, I left my seat and went to my condemnation hearing toolbox and picked up a hard copy of the Iowa Code Section 6B.52 Renegotiation of damages.

This code section was passed when I was working in the Attorney General's office It provided landowners with a permissive five years to renegotiate any unforeseen damage. I gave a copy of the Iowa code section to the first commissioner. He read it while the owner's attorney made the argument that just compensation was now or never. The first commissioner passed the code section on to the second commissioner, and when it got to the last commissioner, the lead attorney picked it up, read it and sat down. He never said another word! He just sat there like he was not even there.

Landowner Legal Council was not finished. The younger attorney called the retired Ames city engineer as a witness and asked if he had reviewed the design of the project. He asked whether the project would work as intended. The engineer said he had reviewed the plans and determined that the project would not work. He identified a couple of technical issues using flood size and velocity words I did not understand. At that point, I asked the City of Tama design engineer to take a minute and talk to the landowner's engineer and make sure that everybody was talking apples and apples and oranges and oranges. That was fun to watch! It took about five minutes. They both nodded their heads in agreement. The landowner's engineer explained what he had learned and what he had no way of knowing. He then determined that the project was functional and that it would work as designed.

Then the younger attorney called his appraiser who estimated just compensation to be twice the amount of the city's appraisal to step up in front of the compensation commission to explain his appraisal. The land sale value proofs he used were three sales of residential home sites in a part of what was the city's golf course. He was comparing golf course home sites to flood-prone farmland. All I had to do was note what his proof was. The commissioners all understood that the landowner's appraiser was incompetent and their use or consideration of his appraisal was improper.

The next witness was Justin Whitzel himself. One of the commissioners moved a chair for him so that he could sit in front of the commission and speak. Justin used his cane and walked slowly to the chair, but when he sat down there was only one cheek on the chair. The other cheek was in midair. It looked for a second like he was going to fall. Two of the commissioners reached out to help him but he finally settled himself on the chair. Justin gave his speech about why he did not want the project. We all left so the commission could deliberate. In about a half an hour, the commission came back with their award and I looked at it.

The award was $4,000 more than the city's appraisal. I couldn't figure out why, so I asked the chairman. The chairman responded: "We were happy with the city's appraisal but Mr. Whitzel had to pay for those assholes." I thought about telling the chairman that the city was responsible to pay any increase over the city's approved appraisal amount. I did not tell him. The chairman was right.

Oops, Let's Do This Again

It did not take long before Murphy's Law made another appearance. No matter how hard you work and how good your intentions are, somehow you can always make a mistake. My staff was busy processing five or six condemnation files on a continuing basis. It was just a matter of time before we made a mistake. We had several condemnation legal descriptions we were processing at the same time. One earlier condemnation legal description for a hearing we had already held had left out a part of some necessary language.

Because of this, it was not clear that the city had acquired all of the land it needed. The nature of the error was also likely to cause a problem in the landowner's record of ownership, or title, that we were probably required to fix at no cost to the city. I waited until after the condemnation award check had been deposited with the sheriff, was picked up and cashed by the landowner and the statutory time to file a condemnation District Court appeal had passed. I then set up the same condemnation again but this time with the correct legal description. The sheriff made service of notice on the landowner and scheduled a new hearing date and time.

On the morning of the hearing, I told the commissioners what had happened and what we were doing and why. I provided a signed copy of their original award and told them that the landowner had cashed his award and the time for appeal had passed. I asked them to return the award of zero dollars so that the proper legal description issue would all be resolved of record and thus not create any title problem for the landowner. The commissioners did as I had asked. They returned an award for zero dollars and the issue was resolved. When I got back to the office everyone cheered. Our GLAA staff took Jane and I out to dinner that night.

The Corps of Engineers Conditional Refusal to Fund Construction

When we took this project, the commanding officer of the Davenport Office of the Corps of Engineers warned us that it had to be completed by a certain date or they would not fund the project's construction. We were a month from that date and still had one key parcel to acquire. This was a commercial business that would be protected by the construction of the flood wall to be located right next to where the business was. We found out when we got into the file for the property that the title search for the parcel was defective. The corporate landowner owned not only the parcel where its business building and workshops were located but also the adjacent bare ground or unimproved property where it stored equipment and materials. The dam was to be built on only a small part of this adjacent unimproved storage parcel.

Neither the appraiser nor the engineer on the project had talked to the adjacent business landowner in the design phase of the project. This was true even though it was clear that the property was not being farmed or used as a property separate from the business. The Tama County courthouse title records showed that someone else owned the adjacent property even though it was the business that was clearly using it. There was also no public record that the business was renting that land from the person who had record title or ownership of the property. If the business really did own the property, the city would be required to reappraise the business's entire assembled property. This would require changing the landowner's legal description and ownership identification. After the property was reappraised, the city would also have to make a new offer to purchase the property before it could even begin the process to condemn the property. None of this could be done in the thirty days left to complete the project.

Once we had all of these facts in place, I visited the commanding officer in Davenport for our monthly face-to-face status report meeting. After waiting for half an hour, I was invited into his highly decorated, very impressive office and, once again I sat down on a chair in front of his desk. We had a cup of coffee and he asked me how the project was going. He knew full well how it was going because I provided weekly status reports to him. With a serious expression, he asked: "What do you think your chances are of getting the last person signed up before the funding deadline a month from now?" He did not know about the title problem for the last parcel. But he knew I could not provide the timely statutorily-required thirty-day notice, hold the condemnation hearing, and meet his absolute deadline. He again explained that he did not have the discretion to grant the city an extra thirty days and wished me luck. I assured him we would do our best to obtain title to the property on time.

When I got back from the Davenport visit, I discussed our options with our acquisition agents. We determined that the only way the project could be funded would be if the last landowner would donate or gift the right-of-way to the project. The minor taking from the adjacent unimproved property did not cause significant damage to the landowner's business operation. It was apparent to me that ultimate just compensation did not involve a lot of money. I set up a meeting with the property owner's corporate board of directors. We went to the meeting with our hat in hand.

I asked the board of directors if they had a copy of the unrecorded deed to the adjacent unimproved property. They said they did. We explained the whole thing to the board. They had several questions. They wanted to know what capital gains

tax would have to be paid. I informed them that there will be
no capital gains on land donated for this public purpose. Most
of the appraised purchase price would likely be paying for the
loss of storage space not presently being used by the business. In
fact, I told the board that it was my opinion that the actual after
the project is completed private commercial market value of the
business would be significantly increased because the flood control
berm was constructed to protect it.

The board was very cordial and invited us to leave the room
while they discussed our request. A half an hour later, they came
out of the boardroom and told us they had agreed to donate the
flood control easement at no cost to the city. They gave us the
original unrecorded deed to the storage parcel they had in their safe
and signed the donation form. I thanked the board for their help.
I told them that I hoped the whole City of Tama appreciated what
they did to assure the completion and construction of the project.

The next day I recorded the lost deed to the property we needed
an easement on in the Tama County courthouse. I also took the
landowner's signed and notarized donation form for the berm site.
I recorded the donation form in the Tama County courthouse and
headed for Davenport. Once again it took a while before I had a
chance to meet with the Corps of Engineer Director. As I sat down
in front of him, he had a sad expression. He told me: "There is
nothing I can do to give the city any additional time."

I told him: "I know what your problem is but we do not need any
more time." I told the Director that we had worked out a donation
with the last property owner, thanked him for his patience and gave
him a copy of the recorded donation form. His BLANK expression at
that moment made that last trip to Davenport a joyful moment. I was
a good boy! I did not break into laughter until I got into my car. When

it was all over, everyone who worked on the project went out to dinner together. We had *more* than just a few laughs and a beer or two.

CITY OF DES MOINES — HUGE SANITARY SEWER PROJECT

G raham Land Acquisition Associates (GLAA) came into being at just the right time for the state of Iowa. This was when statewide, experienced right-of-way engineers, acquisition agents and other key staff all were retiring. Many were not being replaced. In this time frame, from 1991 through1993, the City of Des Moines was threatened with the loss of federal sewer construction funds for a much-needed two-hundred property-owner, multicounty sewer easement acquisition project. Rather than lose their federal funds, the city hired Graham Land Acquisition Associates to acquire the right-of-way. In order to complete the project in a timely manner, we built up (GLAA) negotiator staff. I also hired James T. Hayes Jr., who was Iowa's most experienced eminent domain real estate appraiser and we started to work on the project.

As the project progressed, it was apparent that the appraisal process and negotiations effort were going to be successful. I cannot remember whether we were also doing the title and closing and property owner payment work on this project or whether that was being done by the city. At the same time, because the project was so big, it was necessary to divide it into pieces so that the construction could begin on multiple parts of the project to assure its timely completion. This meant that we had to use the condemnation procedures to acquire one or two easements on several segments of the project. This was true even though almost everything was acquired through a negotiated settlement.

There were always one or two easements that had to be acquired by condemnation to obtain good title or ownership of the easement where landowners did not have clear recorded title to the property needed to construct the sewer line on. This required us to maintain an ongoing condemnation document preparation operation to acquire valid title and ownership of all of the necessary easements.

There were also one or two parcels in each of the several segments where there was no possibility of reaching any settlement. These circumstances were almost always caused by arrogance or greed, or by a deliberate intent to extort the system or a combination thereof. While there were not many of these parcels, these were the parcels that I enjoyed! There were five or six landowners who were always represented by legal counsel and insisted that the matter be resolved in a condemnation proceeding. These contested condemnation hearings were always an uplifting experience! There was one parcel on this project that stood out as being funnier or more devilishly creative than the others.

This special parcel was the April 5, 1991, Mrs. Harbert condemnation where everything went wrong for us. In the Harbert case, the city needed to acquire a narrow twenty-foot-wide, east-to-west, two-acre easement on unfarmed creek-bottom land located along the north property line of her farm. The Harbert farmland sloped upward from north to south and it had an east-west creek on the north property line. The farmhouse was located on the south-side of the parcel at the top of the hill on a county road.

When our negotiator opened communication with Mrs. Harbert, she invited him into the house for a cup of coffee and a cookie. The negotiator explained the project and gave her a copy of the acquisition documents and plat. She indicated that she knew of the project as a result of the public hearing and was interested in what the city's offer was. The negotiator showed her the contract forms.

When she saw the amount the city was offering, she took the coffee and cookie back and told him to leave her kitchen and not to come back until our $4,000 per acre offer was $30,000 per acre. She gave our negotiator the name, address and phone number of her attorney and told him not to bother her again.

Once a week, and sometimes twice a week, for thirty-plus days, our negotiator unsuccessfully tried to contact her attorney. In order to meet construction schedules, a condemnation hearing date was set. Title search for the farmland showed that the farm was partially owned by a person who lived in Illinois who had to be given timely notice of the condemnation hearing by an Illinois sheriff. If I remember right, our only contact with the owner's attorney was by phone and all that was said by the owner's attorney was that the owner wanted $30,000 per acre.

The morning of the very day of the compensation commission hearing, the Illinois sheriff contacted me and informed me that he had not made timely service on the Illinois landowner. I tried to contact the property owner's attorney to tell him the hearing would be delayed. It was too late. He had already left to attend the condemnation hearing at the courthouse.

When we arrived at the courthouse, the six compensation commissioners, the landowner and the landowner's attorney were all there. All I did for an hour was apologize for the delay. We all had to listen to the property owner's attorney explain what an awful and unjust set of circumstances these were. I apologized again and assured them all we would make prompt and correct service of notice and that we would reschedule the hearing without further delay.

When I went back to the office, I contacted the Illinois sheriff and found out that he had made twenty stops over ten days at different times of the day to serve the hearing notices and could never find anyone home. In order to resolve the problem and prevent its recurrence, I gave the service agent a form Notice of Condemnation that had no hearing date on it. I asked the Illinois sheriff to fill in a date by hand that was thirty-five days from the date that he made actual service and delivers it to the Illinois landowner. When the Illinois sheriff finally made service on the Illinois landowner, he called me. We served the Petition for Condemnation on the Iowa landowner on the same day for the same hearing date. It all worked out and we finally had a valid condemnation hearing date.

Then came the second unanticipated disaster. The construction contractor on the creek bottom was supposed to remove junk trees from a property that we already had an easement on. Instead, the contractor removed junk trees from the creek area on the Harbert property. When I found out about the contractor's mistake, I contacted the property owner's attorney and informed him what happened. I set my telephone on the desk so I did not have to hear the scathing non-English words. There was a threat of a separate lawsuit and other things that could not be written down. I told him that the city's appraiser had fully considered the loss of the trees and that he would be fully compensated for them. I do not think I was ever more anxious and looking forward to holding a condemnation hearing than I was to holding this one. I had been talking to James T. Hayes Jr., our appraiser. We thought we had figured out what the landowner's attorney was up to. If we were right, this hearing would really be fun!

When the compensation commissioners viewed the property, the property owner's attorney was there. He pointed out the tree stumps that the city had wrongfully removed prior to the hearing. The key observation that the commissioners made, as far as I was concerned, was that the easement area really had little effect on and did not include any presently tilled or farmed property. Once we got back to the hearing room, I explained the purpose of the project and also explained and apologized for the prior procedural disaster caused earlier by not obtaining valid out-of-state service of notice. The property owner's attorney accepted my apology. He informed the compensation commission that it was the commission's responsibility to justly compensate his client not only for the loss of her property rights but also for all of the increased, unnecessary, unreasonable, and unjust additional costs associated with the city's incompetence.

This all came together very quickly when I asked Jim Hayes to explain the basis for his appraisal and the city's offer. Mr. Hayes gave the compensation commission a copy of his appraisal and told them that this had all been provided to the property owner as part of the negotiations process. He explained the impact of the city's permanent easement rights in the uncropped creek area. He noted that the easement would require some minor directional changes in how the actual crop land was tilled or farmed. Then he noted that he had found three very recent small farm sales with similar uncropped creek area. When he applied these sales prices to the subject property, he determined the basic land value of the farm site per acre and applied these same values to the Harbert property. His basic conclusion was that the farm was damaged by the pipeline easement at $4,000 for the two-acre creek-land easement being acquired.

Before Mr. Hayes could even finish in his analysis, the property owner's attorney jumped out of his seat and quickly moved in front of Mr. Hayes. He asked Mr. Hayes if he knew that the Harberts, just two years ago, had sold a similar easement to the Des Moines Waterworks on the west side of their property adjacent to the road for $30,000 an acre. Mr. Hayes looked directly at him and said: "I was the appraiser for the waterworks $30,000 settlement." Mr. Hayes told the landowner's attorney and the compensation commission: "This Des Moines Waterworks purchase was not a valid comparable free market land sale for eminent domain appraisal purposes. This was because it was not an arm's length, open-market, freely negotiated sale."

At that point the property owner's attorney lost his composure. He stuck his index finger in Mr. Hayes's face and screamed: "Are you an attorney?" Mr. Hayes responded: "No, I am not an attorney, but I am a Certified Real Estate Appraiser and I know that an eminent domain purchase of land needed for a public improvement project is not a free market sale for just-compensation land-valuation purposes." One of the hardest things I have ever done was to just stand there with no expression on my face. When things finally calmed down a little, I asked Mr. Hayes if he had personal knowledge of the waterworks easement purchase. Mr. Hayes informed everyone that he did.

Mr. Hayes said: "I appraised the same property for the Des Moines Waterworks and the same thing happened on the waterworks project that happened on the City of Des Moines's sewer project. Negotiations were delayed and unsuccessful to the point where they were interfering with the actual construction of the waterworks project. I was asked not to appraise the easement but instead to determine the highest price ever paid for any easement for any public purpose anywhere in Polk County. I determined that this was $30,000 per acre. I note coincidentally that this is exactly what the property owner is asking the city to pay for the present sewer easement."

It was over! The property owner's attorney's tactics were unmasked. The award of the compensation commission was exactly what the city had offered, without attorney fees.

The hardest part of successfully dealing with duplicity, arrogance and greed is keeping a smile off of your face and your mouth shut when it is all unveiled for the compensation commission to see. From this point of view, this case was an extremely difficult problem. It might have been harder for Mr. Hayes than it was for me. But we managed to keep our mouths shut until we got to lunch. After a cold beer and all of the laughing finally stopped, things became somewhat semiserious once more. Jim told me that I needed to write Volume 8 Appraising Partial Acquisitions for my Land Acquisition Design courses and offered to help me to do so. I graciously accepted Jim's offer. Jim Hayes's teamtaught Volume 8 with me for ten years. Note my tribute to James T Hayes Jr. in the special March 2013 Land Acquisition Design monthly newsletter. See GrahamLAD.com.

This March 2013 LAD newsletter contains Jim's professional experience resume when he was a condemnation hearing agent for the Iowa State Highway Commission. Mr. Hayes's resume also documents his experience as a negotiator and appraiser for the Iowa State Highway Commission. Jim Hayes left the right-of-way office before I became its Right-of-Way Director for Administration in 1970. The pre-1970 Iowa State Highway Commission Right-of-Way Office dysfunctionality has been reestablished in the present 2015 IDOT Right-of-Way Office. This is all documented in Chapter 10, Managing Land Acquisition Organizations, which is available in its entirety at GrahamLAD.com.

CITY OF JOHNSTON — MERLE HAY ROAD PROJECT

The City of Johnston project was special for a couple of reasons. It's hard to fully understand why this was so without some necessary and relevant background. When our land acquisition company (GLAA) was fully engaged in trying to complete the City of Des Moines Sanitary Sewer and other projects, I had an opportunity to hire two interns. I hoped that maybe Jim Hayes and I could teach them the ropes and thereby expand our informed and skilled negotiation staff. The first intern I hired was David Schatz, who had just graduated from Iowa State University in Ames. The second intern was Ted Francois. My original professional negotiator staff had reservations about David Schatz. They were concerned whether he would be forceful enough to deal with difficult landowners and their aggressive legal counsel.

I was not concerned about it. It was clear to me that David knew where he was, where he needed to go and was quick to determine a plan on how to get there. My observations turned out to be right on the money. David had an endless chain of signed contracts. He helped to validate our company's ability to obtain a negotiated agreement with every person on the project, except occasionally the arrogant and sometimes the greedy. As it turned out, David Schatz's work was a primary reason that Graham Land Acquisition Associates was and continued to be so successful.

I can remember only one time that I totally flummoxed him to the point he did not know what to do. This happened when David and I went to Staples to buy paper and supplies one afternoon. We were both standing inside the door in front of the counter when a middle-aged clerk came up to me and asked if she could help me. While I was in the process of explaining what I needed, a second young *very* good looking clerk came up to me and David. She looked right at David and asked him if she could help him.

Before David could answer her, I told her: "This is David Schatz. David has come to our country from Germany. He was a student at Iowa State University in Ames and he is looking for a wife." David just stood there. He opened his mouth but nothing came out. He did not know what to say. Instead, he turned around and headed for the door. He ended up in front of the indoor, not the outdoor. For a moment he couldn't get out of the store. I may not have laughed any harder at any time in my life but that was the first and only time I ever got him.

The City of Johnston project was no real challenge to David. He signed up every parcel on the project with the exception of three that I apparently had to acquire through condemnation proceedings. David settled two of these properties once he identified and worked out some questioned construction detail. When all of the several owners and their attorneys finally understood what was being built or restored and what was being paid for, David settled those two parcels. The third property could not be settled. The property itself was a single-family home located immediately adjacent to the city headquarters and city engineer's office. The landowner for this residential house was an older woman who was represented by an attorney who identified himself as broadly experienced and extremely successful. No matter how hard and how often David tried, he could not obtain any opportunity to talk to the property owner's attorney.

As the condemnation hearing date got closer, I asked David if he would BEG the property owner's attorney for an opportunity to talk to him. That was where one of Iowa's most accomplished trial attorneys made his mistake. He consented to meeting with David. They finally got together at the last minute the night before the hearing. By this point, the attorney figured that it was too late for the city to effectively deal with any of the issues that he was going to raise at the hearing the very next day. David told the property owner's attorney that he tried to figure out but simply did not understand why this could not be settled. The attorney was not used to dealing with someone quite as slow in understanding as David apparently was. Out of the attorney's professional charity, he took the time to identify three construction-related issues that he stated had not been properly nor clearly documented or explained. Up to this point, we knew nothing about any of these made-up issues. David apologized for his lack of skill and insight and assured him that these things could be worked out.

As soon as David left the attorney's office, he called me and I called the city engineer. The engineer and I worked out a construction statement that was filed the next morning with the compensation commission chairman. The construction statements clarified and resolved the property owner's attorney's issues. The morning of the hearing, the compensation commission viewed the property. The landowner's attorney pointed out these construction problems and noted the financial damage or cost that not fixing them would cause to his client. I didn't say anything more until we got back to the hearing room.

In the hearing, I explained to the compensation commission that these three construction issues were the apparent reason for not being able to settle the case. I apologized to the commission for our not discovering this earlier. Then I gave the commission the construction statements assuring that the work identified in the statement would be done. The landowner's attorney objected. He raised the question whether these agreements were valid. He told the commission that he had not seen any of them in the negotiations process. I reached into my nearby condemnation hearing toolbox. I acted like I was lucky to be able to find an Iowa Supreme Court case that clearly validated the city's right and responsibility to make a filing or record of what was to be built and how it was to be built at a condemnation hearing. You are right. I gave the commission a copy of my 1967 Hinricks v. Iowa State Highway Commission case.

Being the extremely skilled trial attorney that he was, he turned to his backup strategy. He pointed out to the compensation commission that *his mother* lived in the house and that she would be landlocked and unable to get to and from her doctor's office, grocery store, etc. for maybe a month. He noted that none of these additional costs were considered or included in the offer and demanded payment for the full cost of his mother staying in a nearby motel for a month and for some other costs that I do not remember, plus his attorney fees. He gave the chairman his bill for his legal services.

At that point, the city engineer told his mother and the compensation commission that his office was located right next door to his mother's house. He told the attorney that all his mother had to do was call him and he would personally take her directly to wherever she had to go and make sure that she got back the same way. As the commissioners were leaving the room to deliberate, I gave the chairman a copy of David Schatz's time sheet record of his fifteen unsuccessful telephone call attempts to meet with and talk to the attorney.

After the hearing ended, David Schatz and I sat outside the sheriff's office on the benches along the wall on the second floor of the Polk County courthouse waiting for the compensation commission to make their award. All of a sudden, the property owner's attorney came busting out of the office door waving a copy of the award sheet and screaming. He came over to where David and I were sitting. He yelled: "They didn't pay my attorney fees and I had fifteen telephone calls." He didn't wait for an answer. He turned around and started stumbling down the stairs to the first floor of the courthouse. David and I looked at each other. We shrugged our shoulders and went to lunch with a smile on our faces.

David Schatz missed nothing. He came to me just when I needed him. It didn't matter how complicated the issues were or whether it was a legal issue, an engineering issue, an appraisal issue, or an eminent domain process misunderstanding. In every case he asked the questions, researched, and documented the answers for the benefit of property owners and their legal counsel. In my mind, David was the person most likely to be successful as President or Director of my economic development land acquisition company Graham Land Acquisition Associates (GLAA) when I ultimately retired.

The first inkling I had that David Schatz may have another job in his mind was when he bought a house in the Des Moines area. The house was a disaster. It clearly failed to meet the city's decent, safe and sanitary standards. David and his fellow GLAA acquisition agent Ted Francis spent a year restoring the house. While there was nothing unusual in my mind about that activity, what happened next was. Once the work was done he sold the house, or maybe more accurately, *gave* the house to a young homeless family.

I should have known something was up. Shortly thereafter David left GLAA to go take a better job. David became a priest for the Archdiocese of Dubuque. David Schatz may be the most successful recruiter of new priests that the Archdiocese has ever had. It was not until I started thinking about writing *South Hill Rascals* that I put two and two together. I realize now that I have to thank my own namesake Msgr. Emmett Kelly for sending David Schatz to help me when I needed him just as he promised me he would the day before Msgr. Kelly died.

CITY OF ATLANTIC — AIRPORT PROJECT

It is definitely a hard choice, but the City of Atlantic Airport project might have been the most fun I have ever had in making a public improvement project successful. The city hired me to manage the acquisition of the land needed for their project shortly after the completion of the design for the project. There were definitely those in Atlantic that did not want the Atlantic Airport to be improved so that airplanes could land both north to south and east to west and thus be an all-season and all-weather airport.

The project lasted a couple of years as we figured it would. I set the processes up to make sure that the project's development and federal funding approval process clearly followed the requirements of both state and federal law. This would assure that the city would win any failure of procedure lawsuits that may be filed by the landowner. The landowner's attorney, Deborah Peterson, did in fact file two separate lawsuits to stop the project. One suit contested the validity of the city's public hearing and project development requirements. The other suit contested the validity of both the city's and the federal airport funding authority's final approval of the project. The city won them both.

There was even a third District Court suit contesting the validity of the legal description of the land being acquired to expand the airport. This third lawsuit was the property owner's last gasp. The legal description lawsuit claimed that the condemnation legal land description was invalid. A hundred years ago, the first, state land surveyor made a mistake when he established a key corner landmark. This landmark was needed and used by the city to legally describe the actual property being acquired. For this purpose, the law IS and HAS ALWAYS BEEN that the work of the original land surveyor is controlling or final. This original work is, therefore, a valid legal description, all as set out in Volume 4 Land Survey and Property Descriptions of my Land Acquisition Design course.

This was not a normal public works land acquisition project. The existing airport was built upon a huge deposit of a valuable rock or stone. Our landownership title search showed that there was a subsurface stone mining tenant who had a long-term lease under the land being farmed by the landowner and needed for the airport runway expansion. The subsurface tenant had the recorded ownership and right to remove subsurface stone. But in doing so, he had to use a nationally recognized "room-and-pillar" method. This mineral removal method made it possible for the surface landowner to continue to safely farm or otherwise improve and use the surface of the land.

I had some difficulty with the subsurface tenant in reaching an agreement on language stating that the subsurface tenant's, after construction, ownership of mineral rights would be preserved. Once he understood that he could continue to remove and sell the stone, he signed up. His original lease was with the landowner and the city did not disturb that. The city's preservation of the subsurface lease also protected the present private surface landowner's future stone sale income. Another way to put this is that it avoided the city's need to buy out both the landowner's and the subsurface tenant's mineral interests.

Based on the first two property-owner, precondemnation, unsuccessful District Court cases, it was clear to me that the condemnation hearing was going to be SHOW TIME. The city project engineer, appraiser and city administrator Ronald Crisp were all present at the hearing to help explain the need for the project and to defend the city's offer of just compensation. Because of the property owner's attorney's early public meeting and public hearing litigation and public meeting false and half-true claims, I also brought my complete condemnation hearing toolbox to the hearing. This traveling toolbox contained Iowa condemnation and project approval state laws or statutes. It also contained copies of Iowa Supreme court cases approving condemnation procedures and documents needed to identify project design and to reserve land use rights to the owner as a part of the condemnation hearing record.

What the property owner's attorney did not know was that from the beginning to the end of the Atlantic Airport project, I had provided administrative legal advice, research, and assistance but avoided any responsibility to appear in defense of the city in District Court. This made it possible for me to firmly schedule and provide legal assistance to this project and also for other projects that GLAA was providing right-of-way services for. District Court trial work was assigned to Robert Goodwin of Ames. Mr. Goodwin was a former Special Assistant Attorney General to the Iowa State Highway Commission and was familiar with economic development–eminent domain legal issues. Mr. Goodwin and I maintained this relationship for twenty-five years.

In all that time, Mr. Goodwin never lost a landowner's lawsuit contesting the validity of a Graham Land Acquisition Associates project development or acquisition procedure. It was Mr. Goodwin who defended the City of Atlantic in District Court, not me. Deborah Peterson, the landowner's attorney, knew I was involved with the project. However, we had never met one another in a contested proceeding before. I was really looking forward to this condemnation hearing! On the morning of the hearing, Ms. Peterson saw me on the other side of the room and asked me if Bob Goodwin would be here today. With a concerned expression, I told her: "No, Mr. Goodwin couldn't make it. I will just have to have to do my best."

The compensation commissioners all sat behind two tables with their backs against the east wall of the hearing room. There was ample space on the south side of the commission's tables where a separate table was set up for the landowner and the landowner's attorney and witnesses. On the north side of the commissioner's tables, there was another table set up for the city where I sat along with the city's appraiser Brian Linnemeyer, our engineer and Ron Crisp the city administrator. Behind me there was a portable chalkboard on wheels where I kept my all-purpose condemnation hearing toolbox. The entrance to the hearing room from the hallway was in the southwest corner of the room right next to where Ms. Peterson, her witnesses and the landowner sat.

As a commissioner walked into the room, Ms. Peterson rose and greeted the commissioner. I don't think she actually kissed them as they walked in but it appeared to be close. However, each and every time she took the commissioner's hand in hers, she looked him in the eye and thanked him for helping her to be assured that her client would be justly compensated for the *taking* that was to take place that day. And of course, the commissioner assured her he would do so. This happened five times in a row. Each time I simply introduced myself and thanked the commissioner for his help to resolve these issues.

The sixth commissioner was an hour late. When he finally walked through the door, Ms. Peterson also greeted him the same way. As this last commissioner was walking in front of the other seated commissioners toward me, I saw that he had half a smile on his face after this enthusiastic Peterson greeting. My instincts told me that he was looking forward to seeing what this hearing was all about and, more importantly, that he had a sense of humor. I looked right at him with a grin on my face. I simply asked: "What's your excuse?" He looked at me for a second, smiled and told everyone he was calving and just could not get away any sooner that morning. You should have seen the expression of concern on Ms. Peterson's face when it appeared that maybe we knew one another!

After the sheriff introduced everyone and explained the hearing process, he turned the matter over to the chairman of the compensation commission and we all went out to view the property. This included all of the property owner's witnesses and the city's witnesses as well. There were a lot of farming operation changes that had to be made. Most of these changes had to do with a new way the farmer got into the field from adjacent county roads. The project engineer had the plans with him to show the commissioners how farming access, or entrances, worked. Ms. Peterson also had a copy of the condemnation documents, which included a legal description of the land being acquired and an acquisition plat engineering drawing showing the field entrances to the land remaining as part of the farming operation.

Ms. Peterson pointed out that the required formal condemnation petition legal description did *not* include a reference to a farming entrance that would be constructed on one of the remaining county roads. When we got back to the hearing room, I went to my condemnation hearing toolbox and got a copy of my standard form condemnation hearing document Construction Stipulation. The project engineer filled out the location of the missing entrance and the document stated that the entrance would be constructed as designed. We both signed the stipulation and gave the original to the chairman of the commission and a copy to Ms. Peterson.

The first witness was Brian Linnemeyer, the city's appraiser. He did a good job of establishing the basic market value of the farm. I think he had five or six recent sales, all right in the community. He did a really good job of explaining the sales that supported his land value just-compensation conclusion. Ms. Peterson asked Mr. Linnemeyer if he was familiar with how to appraise minerals rights. Mr. Linnemeyer said that he was familiar with the process and started to generally explain what that process was. In his explanation he noted that in the appraisal of mineral rights it was necessary to identify not only the known quantity of material but also their present market value. Ms. Peterson cut Mr. Linnemeyer off. She did not ask him why he had not appraised the mineral rights. I never said a word.

I could not believe how lucky I might be if Ms. Peterson was claiming a right to compensated for the landowner's *false* future loss of mineral income. Ms. Peterson later did tell the commissioners that the city's appraisal was illegal. She claimed that Mr. Linnemeyer should have included a before and after estimate of the value of the whole property including the minerals. Then Ms. Peterson again asked Mr. Linnemeyer if he even knew how to appraise mineral interests. Mr. Linnemeyer told her that he did know and once more started to explain what the process was. Ms. Peterson cut him off again before he could finish his explanation.

When I finished the city's appraisal-related, just-compensation presentation, Ms. Peterson got up and made her arguments. She presented a copy of what she said was an appraisal of the property that included a valuation for both surface farming rights and for mineral rights on all of the land being acquired for the airport. If the compensation commission returned an award in the amount that Ms. Peterson asked for, it would more than double what the city was offering. I knew that this was going to take half an hour or more before she finished her presentation.

I got to thinking about how I could help to expose her misinformation to the commission. She was not asking for just compensation for damages to the farming operation, which was all that was being acquired. She was also asking for a present payment for lost profit caused by the nonexistent loss of mineral rights under the city's new airport runway. My Irish nature told me that the best way to deal with this kind of an issue was to have fun with it.

When Ms. Peterson rose and began talking about her client's rights, I started to look through two piles of document resources I had sitting on the table next to me. I acted like I was not listening to her but was looking for something I desperately needed. I knew I had plenty of time. From what I had heard from Bob Goodwin in the two earlier District Court cases, Ms. Peterson always had much to say. She took her time so that everybody understood what her message was. I acted like, for some reason, I could not find what I was looking for in either document pile next to me. With a very concerned expression, I left the table and went behind the portable chalkboard and pulled out my emergency tool kit. This was a plastic box the size of a full box of reamed typing paper. Its contents were subdivided sixty times with labeled dividers. I looked through the toolbox three or four times for about five minutes. I did this two separate times while she was talking.

Half of the compensation commission was looking at my desperate effort. The city administrator, Ronald Crisp, had a *horribly* concerned expression on his face. Finally, I went back to the table. Ms. Peterson started talking about uncompensated for damages because the city failed to provide the needed farming entrances. She noted that the city appraiser had, in fact, considered that the omitted entrance would be built in his appraisal. She noted that the actual condemnation documents failed to provide for the entrance. At that point, I again became visibly agitated and went back to the toolbox. What no one in the room knew was that I already had everything I needed. When Ms. Peterson finished her presentation, I stood up and informed the commission that I would like to provide a response to the issues that she raised. I took one issue at a time.

I told the commission there were two things they needed to know about the mineral rights issue. The first was that the city was neither taking nor damaging the landowner's right to future mineral income. I gave the chairman a copy of the city's signed and recorded nonacquisition agreement with the subsurface tenant. This agreement preserved surface landowner mineral income rights on the land acquired by the airport authority for runway purposes to the sole use and benefit of the present landowner. It also preserved the subsurface tenant's right to continue to mine minerals after the airport project had been completed. I explained that this was why the appraiser was not required to appraise the value of the mineral interests for eminent domain just compensation purposes. The commonsense reason for this was that all mineral interests would continue to be owned by the landowner even after the landowner's surface rights were acquired for the airport runway expansion project.

In support of the city's appraisal process, I gave the commission a recent Iowa Supreme Court how to value mineral rights case. I told the commission that Ms. Peterson's claim that mineral rights should have been valued both before and after the acquisition in the appraisal was false. Her claim was inconsistent with and was directly repudiated by the simple fact that no mineral interests were being acquired from anyone. I told the commissioners that the whole issue of how to appraise mineral rights was an intentional smokescreen. The simple answer was that the city was not taking or damaging any of the landowner's future mineral income.

I also told the commission of the city's construction stipulation amendment to the condemnation reserving the farming entrance that was inadvertently omitted from the legal description in the condemnation documents. The commissioners knew that the stipulation assuring that the entrance would be built was the just and reasonable thing to do. I told the commission that it also needed to prevent unnecessary and unintended damages to the remaining farming operation. In support of this, I furnished a copy of another Iowa Supreme Court case that validated similar condemnation hearing legal description changes reserving property or property rights to landowners. You guessed it, it was the Hinrichs case.

As we were all leaving the hearing room, Ms. Peterson stood up. She had a neutral expression as she walked over to the chairman's document pile. She looked at the county road farming entrance reservation document. She acted as if she had never been given a copy of the document before the hearing started. She also looked at the Supreme Court case copies I had given to the chairman. She said nothing and left the room with the landowner to take a seat in the hallway outside the room.

It took about a half an hour for the compensation commission to return the award of damages. Ronald Crisp, the city administrator, and I were also waiting in the hallway. It was not long after the commissioners closed the door on the hearing room that we heard some sustained and not so muted laughing inside. It took the commission just a half an hour to return their award. The just-compensation award was exactly what the city had offered, plus a couple of hundred dollars for something that I can't remember. After we had both received a copy of the commission's award, I thought I heard Ms. Peterson whisper under her breath: "Oh dung!" I smiled and fancied myself drawing a puff from my leprechaun pipe.

We all left the courthouse with a smile but no one said anything until we got to the local café for lunch. The people at the café must have thought we were crazy! We laughed and yelled and carried on for half an hour before we all ate, shook hands. I went home with a smile on my face.

Twenty years later, I got a telephone call from Ronald Crisp who told me that he was retiring. He just called to remind me and thank me for his memory of this condemnation proceeding. He said that he has told this story a hundred times and still laughs every time he thinks about it. I thanked him for his telephone call and wished him well in his retirement. No acquiring authority Economic Development–Eminent Domain attorney can ask for more than that!

CHAPTER 12—THE FAMILY THAT PLAYS TOGETHER STAYS TOGETHER

I think our whole Graham family has always had an interest in flying. This goes back to the time when my sons Harry, Dan, Charlie and Matthew and I built our Graham scale-model-airplane collection. When I think about it, it goes farther back than that for me. It was not until the Loras Academy rifle team taught me that I did not have good enough eyesight to be a pilot that I kind of gave up on the idea. Charles Joseph my third son was our primary Graham pilot. Charlie flew for the 128th Air Refueling Wing, Wisconsin Air National Guard, stationed in Milwaukee, Wisconsin. Charlie flew combat and combat support missions in 3 foreign wars and multiple contingency operations worldwide. He was an instructor pilot flying the KC-135R Stratotanker primarily for air refueling operations. Charlie retired after 24 years of service with a Wisconsin Air National Guard as Lt. Colonel. He now flies as a pilot for Delta Air Lines. My brother, Joseph Harry Graham, also earned his wings as a pilot and has had the fun of flying and owning two high-wing light airplanes.

Taking the whole Graham family to the Oshkosh, Wisconsin, Antique Airplane Annual Air Show was, and is, a normal thing for the Graham family to do. We did it as often as we could. I smile when I think of the following typical happenings.

Ariel, our son Matthew's first child, was four or five years old and in a bad mood early in the morning as we pulled up into the parking lot of the air show. I drove a four-door Pontiac that had a hole in the backseat for the armrest that a little person could crawl through if the person was flexible enough. We all got out of the car and closed its passenger doors. A minute or so later someone had observed that we had left things in the car. I reached for the keys in my pocket. I could not find them. Then there was someone who saw that there were keys in the ignition. What would we do? Then I got the idea that maybe Ariel could climb through the open trunk go through the backseat armrest and save the day. That is exactly what she did! We all thanked Ariel and everyone including Ariel had a wonderful time that day. I had a spare key just in case.

We always spent a lot of time looking at the really old airplanes. My wife Jane fell in love with the 1930s R-1 Bee Gee Racer. All day long everyone would try to decide what the best old airplane at the show was. For Jane, it was always the Bee Gee.

For me one of the funniest times at the Oshkosh Air Show was when everyone in the huge crowd watched the live airshow. Son Dan's oldest son, Ryan, and I went up to the snack bar, I thought to get some cold pop. What Ryan really wanted was a BIG ice cream cone. I told Ryan that it was too hot and he would never be able to eat it before it melted all over him. Ryan insisted that was nonsense and asked me again. I thought about it and ordered the triple decker ice cream cone. We had to walk through the whole crowd to get back where the family was sitting. It must've taken us fifteen minutes to get there. Ryan had ice cream ALL over him. Luckily, he missed dropping any of the ice cream on other visitors. I asked Ryan if he knew where the water fountain was so he could wash up and he acknowledged that he did. I still smile when I think of it.

One of the most amazing airplanes on display was the World War II, German, three-engine transport plane known as the Junker JU-52. Harry's son Kevin James fell in love with the JU-52 and we *all* had a ride in it. There was one time when Chuck Yeager, one of America's most renowned World War II Mustang fighter pilots, flew into the air show in the most beautiful North American P 51B Mustang I have ever seen. I took son Charlie's picture with Chuck Yeager standing on the side of his beautiful Mustang. They both have big smiles!

The plane that interested me and my brother Joe the most was the 1930s Ford Trimotor airliner with a third engine on its nose just like the German World War II, JU-52 transport plane. Neither Joe nor I could resist taking a ride in the Ford Trimotor.

I remember another air show when we saw this huge brand-new US Air Force cargo plane land on the air show's runway. It slowly taxied up to where it could be seen by the crowd. This all happened at the end of the first day of the show. When we got back to the show the next day we saw that this huge cargo plane was parked where everybody who was watching the airshow could walk through it. As we got close, the plane's pilot yelled, "Hey, Charlie!" When we got to the plane, the pilot and Charlie hugged one another. Charlie introduced the pilot as one of the pilots in his Air Force flight training class. Needless to say, we all got an in-depth inspection and explanation of the new airplane.

One of my dreams was to build and fly in a World War I, Nieuport-17, single-engine, single-seat, two-winged biplane fighter plane. Over time, I got a copy of the complete set of plans to build it, along with a list of all of the materials. I bought some of the tools needed to do so. When I started writing the first Land Acquisition

Design course I also designed and had a trailer built to carry the Nieuport 17. As was the case with the original 1916 biplane, the wings could be removed and hung on the side of the trailer. This is where the Graham family scale-model-airplane collection was stored. Maybe someday the Graham family will find a place to display the collection so the public can enjoy this unique and wonderful airplane model collection.

MISSISSIPPI RIVER RATS AT PLAY

I can't remember the exact year when my brother Joe and his wife Ruth first worked together with the whole Frentress Lake community to set up the lake's first Fourth of July community parades. That was one of the better ideas that the Fentress Lake community ever had. Mothers pulled their dressed-up little kids in wagons and grownups walked, dressed as anything or as anyone. Neighbors and their holiday visiting family drove and rode in the parade on anything with four or two wheels, or one wheel, with everyone painted up or in costume. The fire trucks sprayed the kids in the crowd and the police cars blared their sirens. The little kids watching the parade ran up and down and all over picking up candy that was thrown by people all dressed up and riding in their fancy decorated wagons, trucks and everything else. For many years, before the parade got so big, after the parade was over the north neighbors had a big lunch all set out on tables in their backyards. In the first few years of the parade there was even backyard after-lunch entertainment.

George Washington Crossing the Delaware
My brother Joe, his wife Ruth, Gini and Jim Apple, Rod Zaff, John Flynn and other neighbors all put together an after-parade Frentress Lake George Washington-crossing-the-Delaware play. It was Gini

Apple, an elementary school teacher, who had a great interest in American history who came up with the original idea. Looking back at it, I think Washington crossing the Delaware was the goofiest and most fun of all of the Fourth of July Frentress Lake after parade celebrations. My brother Joe assembled three rowboats so George Washington's army could cross the lake from the riverside for the attack on the Apple cottage. Sons Dan and Charlie and I were each in separate boats. Each boat was filled with older and obviously more mature cousins, and they all carried BB guns.

Everyone was dressed in American Revolutionary war uniforms. I was dressed as George Washington. Brother Joe was the key for us obtaining the uniforms. Joe donated outdated blue prom tuxedos for the American patriots and fiery red tuxedos for the British. Rod Zaff was the British general Cornwallis. Cornwallis could be identified because he wore a crowned majorette headdress.

The British fort was defended by Rod Zaff's British Redcoats. The Redcoats were fortified behind protective barriers on both the Apple dock, which stuck out into the lake, and on the lakeshore beach yard. Dressed as George Washington, I stood up in the front of the first rowboat just like the real George Washington did. We began VERY SLOWLY rowing across Frentress Lake toward the British fort. The Redcoats set up their first defensive positions with their BB guns on the Apple cottage boat dock. It all sounded good to hear BBs bouncing off of our three metal rowboats. All you could hear from both the boats and from the fortified dock was *ping, ping, ping, ping*.

Then the Redcoats made a mistake. They hit son Dan's open beer can in his rowboat and spilled it. At that moment things got serious. Son Charlie's rowboat swung to the left while son Dan's rowboat swung to the right of my boat. We all opened fire on the Redcoat's dock defenses. Grahams know how to shoot BB guns! It did not take long to drive the Redcoats off of the dock where they took up their last-ditch defenses behind an over turned rowboat on the beach.

When George Washington's invading army got close enough to where the Bluecoats could not miss, the Redcoats gave up. The whole assembled Frentress Lake audience cheered! All the Redcoats gave up except Rod Zaff. Rod ran up to my wife, Jane, in the middle of the whole audience and tried to take Jane as a prisoner. Rod made a desperate move, all in friendly jest. He grabbed my wife in a bear hug and lumbered off a few steps. Janie screamed from his unexpected clutch. Janie yelled: "Hey, wait a minute! We won this war! You get back to England!" When that happened, Jane rained multiple blows on Rod's chest, much to the laughter of the entire crowd. Jane's informal picture shows the Victorious Blue Coats.

Katie's "Chia" Car

One of the best entries ever made in the Fourth of July parade was made by my brother Joe's daughter, Kathryn Graham (now McFadden). Katie and Rebecka Brown, one of Katie's longtime lake friends, took an old car and turned it into a moving, giant, growing flower. I am not sure how they permanently packed two-inch thick river mud on the trunk, the top, the hood and on all four fenders of the car. Katie told us it took a month to get it all to grow and blossom so it would be ready for the Fourth of July parade. They did such a good job that the whole Frentress Lake parade was featured in the *Dubuque Telegraph Herald*, complete with a picture of the "Chia" car.

Brother Joe with Nine Up on Water Skis

In the afternoon after the parade and the play or other activities were over, my brother Joe and his sons, my sons, my brother Tom's sons, my brother John's son and a daughter and lake neighbor kids all dressed up as girls and in other nonsense stuff. No one knew if this was going to be a successful effort to make my brother Joe's year-after year attempt to get nine people up on water skis at one time. Maybe that partially explains the way everybody was dressed up.

Power was not the problem. Joe's Mastercraft speedboat was specifically designed to make this all possible. The lineup of the skiers was so wide that getting started from the beach in a straight line direction was just the beginning of the problem. Once everyone was up, the left side of the line of skiers had to turn hard left to be able to maintain enough speed to stay up. At the same time the right side of the line of skiers had to lean back to stay with the speed of the boat so that they all could turn left and go south down Frentress Lake in a straight line. The year it actually happened, my wife, Jane, got the picture. This wonderful picture proves that they actually made it. What the picture does not show is that thirty seconds after everyone was up and skiing three skiers dropped off. Even so, the picture still tells the truth. This amazing picture hangs in the first floor of Joe's new Graham cottage. No one knows if the next generation of Grahams will be able to do that again.

Frentress Lake's Golden Girls

For several years the Graham family's great-grandmothers always had a front seat to watch the Fourth of July parade and all of the nonsense that went on in front of the cottage and on the lake itself after the parade. They were both referred to as the Golden Girls sitting in the front seat. These much-loved Golden Girls included my brother John's mother-in-law, Pearl Fink, and my wife's mother, Betty Pope. Every time I think about the two of them sharing their wonderful stories with one another and with everyone else all day, it brings a smile to my face. Both Grandma Pearl and Grandma Betty did everything they could to help with the cooking for as long as they could. For as long as they could physically get into brother Joe's Mastercraft speedboat, Joe always took both of the Golden Girls for a boat ride around the lake or up the river.

There was one Fourth of July parade time when Grandma Betty dressed up as Cleopatra. She got a dust mop broom head, dyed it black and wore it for her hair. Jane told me that her wig was completed with a golden cobra-head crown. She made her full-length queenly gown out of fancy golden cloth all tied together with a big, black belt. Everyone knew she was supposed to be Cleopatra, as she pointed her 4-foot long black staff of authority at the crowd while walking in the parade.

Maybe Grandma Betty's best outfit was when she dressed up as Scarlet O'Hara. She used a green velvet window drapery and draped it over a window curtain rod across her shoulders for her dress. She did this even though the afternoon temperature was 100°F! In the movie, Scarlet was getting dressed to see Rhett Butler because she needed $300 to pay taxes on Tara, her family plantation. All along the parade people pointed at Betty and knew she was dressed as Carol Burnett's Scarlet O'Hara and laughed. That was the year that the *Telegraph*

Herald reporter talked to Betty and took a picture of her, but it was Katie Graham's Chia car that got the attention in the paper.

To me, the funniest Golden Girls story had nothing to do with the Frentress Lake parade. Instead it had to do with my brother Joe giving everyone a Mastercraft ride on tires and inner tubes. There was always a demand to pull the little kids in the water on big truck-tire inner tubes. Some of the earlier tires were big enough so that two kids could be in them or hang on to them at the same time. Joe would pull them around the lake as fast as he could while still giving them a chance to hang on as the tire would literally skip across the surface of the lake. The kids soon learned to keep both legs in the water as a kind of a rudder. If they didn't do that, the tire would skip across the water and sometimes turned completely over. When that happened, the kids ended up under the tire instead of on top of it. In pulling kids, you had to be a little bit careful for a while until they figured out that you were telling them the truth when you told them how to do it.

Giving the kids a ride on the tire went on for many years. It didn't take long before the truck tire inner tube was replaced by an actually designed flatter plastic tube. The new fancy plastic tube had handholds built into it. It was actually designed so you could skip across the surface of the water. If you were riding the new tube, it was in your best interest to know how to keep your legs and feet in the water to both steer and slow the speed of the tube in turns. If you were not smart enough to keep your feet in the water, you could actually pass the speedboat when the boat was turning. If you passed the speedboat, two seconds later the boat would catch up and the slack in the rope would snap straight. No matter how strong you were, if this happened it would rip you off of the tube. When you and the tube parted company, it was in your best interest to keep your mouth shut rather than scream at the boat's driver. That was the best way to avoid swallowing large quantities of water.

It sometimes took brother Joe an hour or two to give all the little kids and any of the ladies a ride on the new tube. For example, we have a good picture of Jane and I in separate tubes tubing side-by-side down the lake. In the beginning, the younger riders tried to stay away from one another as they speeded up and down the lake. This went on until they learned to steer the tube by directing their feet in the water. Their feet became the rudder that they used to steer with. It was fun to watch the little kids as they learned to steer their tubes. Sometimes they deliberately would run into the other person to see what would happen. Other times they tried to steer as far to the right or the left side of the speedboat as they could. While that was fun for the young ones, it never got serious and the boat was not going as fast as it could to begin with.

There was one tubing time that will stick in my mind forever. It was also one of the funniest Golden Girls events that ever happened at our Graham Fourth of July Frentress Lake family gatherings. It all happened in the middle of the afternoon after brother Joe had taken care of all the younger tube riders. As I remember it, Joe was driving his Mastercraft with a full boatload of guys who were going to try the high-speed stuff after the little kids and girls had their rides. Joe's son Ben was in the boat, as was brother Tom's son Bob and brother John's son Mike. I sat at the very back of the boat in the right corner. Grandma Betty sat in the very back of the boat opposite of me in the left corner. Both Grandma Betty and I could reach over the side of the boat and touch the water that was just a foot and a half below us.

Ben, Bob and Mike all sat together in the middle of the boat in front of the engine. This was close to where brother Joe was driving the boat. As the day went on, Mike told Bob that it did not matter how fast the boat was going that he could not be thrown off the tube. He reckoned that was because of his advanced physical skill and balance. For some reason Bob did not accept Mike's statement at face value and told him that he could dump him anytime he wanted to. Brother Joe was sitting close enough to both of them so that he heard what they were saying. Apparently Joe was willing to test the question and agreed to allow Bob to drive the boat to see what would actually happen. Neither Grandma Betty nor I heard any of this until later as we were sitting behind the engine in the back of the boat just enjoying the ride and the wind in our faces on the hot day.

As soon as Bob was able, he took control of the boat and had Mike in the back on the tube. This was a totally different ride. The Mastercraft approached forty-five miles per hour and stayed there throughout the entire ride. When we got down to the south end of the lake Bob swung the boat east to obtain enough room for a high-speed turn to the west to be sure the lake was wide enough for Mike to complete his turn in the water and not crash onto the island that separated the lake from the river. Mike had both feet deep in the water and stayed as far away from the boat so he could to keep the tow rope straight. Much to everyone's amazement Mike stayed up on the tube! Bob kept the boat at full speed and swerved HARD LEFT trying to create some slack in the rope and then quickly HARD RIGHT as we flew north up the lake. Each time Mike successfully countered with a wolfing move in the opposite direction.

When we got to the Graham cottage, Bob did not stop to allow Mike to declare victory. Instead he made another highest possible speed turn. Mike anticipated the turn and survived it again. Bob had the boat flying south again. This time he turned the boat right instead of left when he got to the south end of the lake. The first time we made the south end turn my right side rear seat was only two inches above the water itself. If the boat had been ten miles an hour faster the water may have come in the boat all over me. This time the turn was left and I am sure that Grandma Betty saw that she could also have put just her hand over the side of the boat and touch the water. Unfortunately for

241

Bob, Mike survived both the right-hand turn and the full-speed zigzag race back north to the cottage.

When we got back to the Graham dock and tied the boat up, I heard Bob say that he did not remember that Grandma Betty was in the back of the boat. After I heard Bob say that, I asked Ben: "What do you think Bob would've done if he had known that Grandma Betty was in the boat?" Ben answered with a smile: "He would probably have apologized more." I asked Grandma Betty how she felt about that ride. Her answer was beautiful! Grandma Betty told me: "I thought to myself that Graham boys have done such crazy things all their lives and have managed to survive. *I thought I would probably survive so* I might just as well sit back and enjoy the ride." She laughed when brother Joe told her that there was nothing for her to worry about because he would have saved her. Those who know Grandma Betty know that she is both loving and smart but a little bit on the play-it-safe side. Many years later when I reminded Grandma Betty of this event, she got a big smile on her face and told me the whole thing again word for word.

King of the Boat Dock

As long as I can remember, the Graham dock was the location of intergenerational Fourth of July holiday warfare or maybe I should say "playfare." I think the idea itself started with my brother Tom and I and our mother's brother, Uncle Jack Schiltz. Uncle Jack kept throwing Tom and me off the Graham dock or off Jack's dock, which at that time was only three feet away from our dock on the lake. It didn't take Tom and me long to catch on. If Uncle Jack dropped his guard, he ended up in the water whether he liked it or not. When my kids and brother Tom's kids became adults (whatever that is for a Graham), every kid on the lake came to do their best to throw them off of brother Joe's dock. After that, there was no way to control it.

This always happens either right after lunch or right after dinner when everyone was full of energy. The best picture we ever took of this nonsense was one where my sons Matthew and Harry and brother Tom's son Ed were trying to defend themselves on the dock. There was a line of their attackers waiting to be thrown off the dock that extended twenty feet up the beach itself. This wonderful picture also still hangs in brother Joe's new Graham cottage. When Graham grandkids win control over the dock, they will be the fourth generation of Graham's to play "King of the Dock."

The Cardboard-Boat Race

I think it was brother Joe's son Ben who came up with the idea of having a cardboard boat race. Many of the Graham Clothing Store boxes that men's and women's suits and clothes came in were huge. Even so it must've taken months to accumulate all the cardboard needed to build the twelve boats that entered the race. This was not just a Graham family event. Adjacent cottage owners, their kids and visiting family also built a cardboard boat and entered the race. Contestants picked up their cardboard and roll after roll of strong black duct tape early in the morning. Who knows how each contestant came up with the design for their boat? Everyone built his or her boat at a different location. Once built, there was no boat that looked like any other boat, as each boat was totally unique in its design and appearance. I wish I could remember all the names that everyone painted on their boats. I remember one was painted titanic. This for sure turned out to be appropriate. It never made it out as far as the end of the dock. When all the boats were assembled on the beach the builders took pictures of their finished boats. Everyone gave their pilots their last rites, just in case.

Some of the contestants used little kids as their boat pilot in order to save weight and hopefully to increase speed. It was fun to listen to the boat owners trying to explain to the little kid why they were *not* going to sink into the water. I heard one boat builder explain to their young pilot that the reason the pilot had to wear a life preserver was because it was a law that racing boat pilots had to wear a life preserver. I heard four or five boat builders telling their little kid pilot that if he or she won the race they would pay him or her five dollars. All they had to do was to get into their boat on the shore and race out less than fifty feet to the float at the end of the dock and turn around. The first boat to reach the shore again obviously won the race. It took all morning and half of the afternoon before everyone was actually ready to start the race.

All the boats were in the water next to the shoreline. Everyone was watching the race starter on the Graham dock, waiting for him to give the go signal. Each boat had a pusher to give their boat a good start. The signal came and everyone pushed off. Three of the ten boats didn't get five feet out into the water before they started to tilt in one direction or another. The pilot tried to use his or her paddle to correct the tilt and still move out into the lake. It did not work. Another eight or ten feet went by and three or four more boats started to tilt and tip over. When the boats actually got out to the end of the dock and turned around to come back there were only two boats left. Brother Joe's daughter Katie was in one of the boats. Katie was the only boat that actually finished the race. The second boat finished the race too but it did not count because its pilot was carrying the boat, not riding in it.

There must've been a hundred people watching this goofy race. They all were breaking up laughing from the very beginning of the race to its ultimate sinking end. After all the pilots were rescued, we discovered why brother Joe's daughter Katie won the race. I had looked over all the boats as they were being constructed and every one of them was thoroughly taped and put together as solidly as they could possibly be. Then as I looked over the winning boat, I noticed it was starting to come apart. This was not one boat. It was two boats with one built on top of the other! Katie had twice the chance to succeed as anyone else and she did. There has been some recent talk that maybe we ought to do that again.

Beanbag-Throw Tournament

Every year, when the water level in the river will allow it, the Graham family holds a Frentress Lake beanbag-throw championship. This is not just a Graham family annual contest. All the nearby Frentress Lake cottages and their visiting families contribute as victims or contestants in the tournament. While all this nonsense is going on—shortly after the Frentress Lake parade—the rest of the visiting family, neighbors and friends were swimming, boat riding, playing cards, or just visiting.

There have been as many as four separate beanbag games going on at the same time side-by-side. As one team got beat and had to drop out, another team would step in and take its place. There were always sixteen guys and girls playing at the same time. The teams that got beat would just shuffle their membership to make up a new team. Then they would go right back into play. This whole process goes on until it started to get dark. The only thing that would stop it earlier would be if there was a clear winner. The idea of a clear winner is a deceptively simple term. What I should have said was a clear winner in accord with Graham Fentress Lake beanbag rules.

For example, once a game started, no member of either team could leave the game until the game was over. The only exception to this was if a contestant had to go to the bathroom. In that case, he or she had to comply with the three-minute-return rule. Some chose the lake and some chose the cottage as a relief resource. This rule was not as bad as it sounds. Remember, there are three other persons playing the game and it takes each person about two minutes to throw both bags. The three-minute rule is more like a nine-minute rule. The other practical consequence of this stay-and-play rule is that it is necessary for each team to have a third person who would provide the players with coffee, cookies or beer whenever it was needed.

No one can really succeed at this game unless they also know the local rules of the game. Some of the minor variations from international rules include the following:

1. The FOUR-BAGGER RULE is where one team member throws four successive bags for that particular round into the hole. This is a perfect score, so to speak. This results in an automatic victory regardless of anyone else's score or lead going into the round. After a four bagger is thrown at Frentress Lake everyone's eyes grow very large. " FOUR-BAGGER!" is screamed and everyone playing in ALL FOUR games must jump into the lake. The two players on the team who throw the four-bagger also receive an opportunity to memorialize the occasion by initialing and dating the bottom of the board with a magic marker. One of the practical consequences of the four-bagger rule is that all players must leave their watches and wallets on the table on the beach. It is against the rules to allow players to stop somewhere to protect his wallet and watch or to change cloths.

2. The ALL-TIED-UP RULE is where your team score settles at 20 after the end of your round. If this happens, your score slides back down to the opposing team's score. Where your opposing team score is 12 your score is now 12. There are times when the smart beanbag player will throw away his second bag in order to avoid the all-tied-up rule. There are other times when the score is 20 and it is absolutely necessary for the second throw to land on the board for the 21st game winning point to avoid the all-tied-up rule.

3. The NUCLEAR SCORE RULE is where your team score slides back to ZERO, if after the end of a round your score is 13. The only good thing that happens to the victim of this rule is if they scored last they get to start with the first throw of the next round. I am not sure how much sense that makes. Maybe that's the point. It gives you something to argue about. :-)

Final Question

Now that you finished the book, ask yourself, what parts do you think were possibly overstated? Notice my careful choice of words. If you conclude that the answer is NONE, you are **right.** For this, the Graham family is eternally grateful.

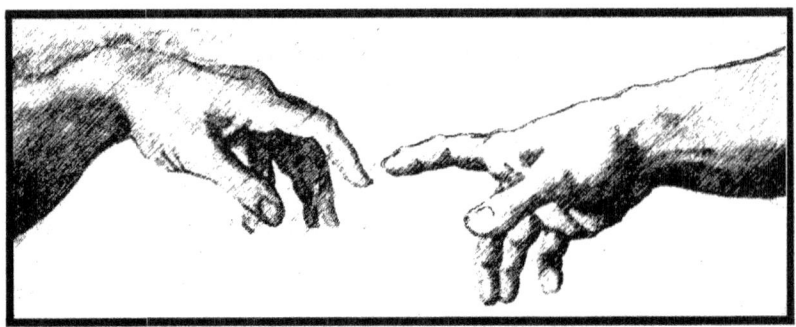

GRANDPA JIM'S PRAYER

O LORD, Thank You for our loving playful family and for the creative work You have given me, and all of us to do.

THANK YOU and please guide us to do Your Will and Give us all the faith and courage to be who You made us to be.

HELP OUR YOUNG ONES to know that by their becoming who You mean them to be, they will always have Your help.

LET THEM LIVE IN THE CONFIDENCE that all of God's children who seek Him, will find Him.

LET THEM KNOW that in finding You, we will all always be together. ☺

The Dubuque Grahams have worked together and played together since 1901 when my grandfather Edward Francis Graham first worked in downtown Dubuque at Boston Clothiers and then Kraft Clothing in 1921. The Graham clothing name started in 1968 when the store became Graham Style Store. One hundred and fourteen years and 4 generations later, the Grahams still work together and still play together at their Fentress Lake cottage every Fourth of July holiday. As my father, Joseph Gill Graham, would say: "That's the way it should be!"

JAMES GRAHAM
6TH *Duke of Montrose*
MARY LOUISE
Daughter of
12th Duke of Hamilton

ONCE AGAIN
OVER GREENER HILLS
WE RIDE FOREVER
YOU AND ME

CHAPTER 13—GRAHAM HERITAGE EPILOGUE—ABOUT THE AUTHOR

I provided the following summary of my professional life at my 1964 Iowa Law School fifty-year class-reunion dinner. The conversation at the dinner focused on much of the fun and nonsense that the class of 1964 all experienced in law school. Several class members and I also furnished individual biographical work summaries similar to the following.

IOWA LAW SCHOOL 1964-2014, fifty-year class dinner, 201 S. Lynn St., Iowa City, Iowa.

1. At married student housing, fishing in the river just below the old law school in1964, in Iowa City with all the neighbor kids bringing my uncleaned, fresh-caught live catfish home to their parents. Don't you wonder what their parents reaction was?

2. Fifty years exclusive Economic Development-Eminent Domain practice of law beginning with four years as Assistant Attorney General for the Iowa State Highway Commission.

3. Twenty years as Right-of-Way Director—Administration for both the Iowa State Highway Commission and the Iowa Department of Transportation.

   • For several years prior to 1991 the Iowa Department of

Transportation right-of-way office was the most efficient in the Midwest.

- Participated in the drafting and implemented both the initial and the second version of Iowa statutory law, the first two versions of Iowa Administrative Rules and ISHC Right-of-Way Office policy and procedure manuals to implement Iowa Code Chapter 6B Procedure under eminent domain and Chapter 316 Relocation of Persons Displaced by Highways required to comply with the national Uniform Relocation Assistance and Property Acquisition Policy Act.

4. Established and directed Graham Land Acquisition Associates, Inc. for twenty years.

- Authored ten Land Acquisition Design [LAD] courses. See course outlines on GrahamLAD.com.

- Taught the first nine of the ten LAD courses to a thousand Iowa multilicensed professionals.

- Authored and taught LAD course Volume 6 Railroads this is the only course in the nation on railroad right-of-way. Drafted and promoted new legislation that was passed to clarify ownership of abandoned railroad right-of-way easements.

- Made co-contributed to current Iowa Department of Transportation Right-of-way Appraisal Manual, 2013.

- Twenty-year effort trying to promote a fix to the current legal maladministration of the Iowa Department of Transportation's broken post-1990 right-of-way administration, acquisition, condemnation, relocation assistance, and property management systems.

5. Coauthored and instructed with Prof. Emeritus Rud Lubson, the Land Acquisition Design (LAD) Volume 4, Land Survey and Property Descriptions

- Provided the Iowa legislature legal analysis of proposed legislative bill that would, if passed, destroy the land survey profession by removing all professional responsibility for land surveyors. It did not pass.

6. Trying to find a way to pass on the original LAD courses and their updating monthly newsletters to a whole new generation of Iowa attorneys, engineers, land surveyors and other state licensed professionals.

   - Chair, Iowa State Bar Association, Government Practice Section 2011–2012.

   - Offering all ten LAD courses including updating monthly LAD Newsletters and Condemnation Appeal manuals and identified Land Acquisition Design library resources to the Iowa State Bar Association for multilicensed professional continuing education programing.

7. Published complete LAD Volume 10 Managing Land Acquisition Organization text in 2013, which is available in its entirety as a part of the GrahamLAD.com website.

   - Volume 10 identifies the Iowa Economic Development–Eminent Domain system's present dysfunctionality. It explains its cause and recommends necessary statutory revisions to fix the current system and to prevent its recurrence. LAD monthly 2009–2014 newsletters identify IDOT administrative and system deficiencies. This information will benefit both state and local acquiring authorities attempting to implement public works projects. It will also greatly assist landowners to identify what their legal and procedural rights are on current public improvement projects.

   - Introduced Volume 10 to the Iowa State Bar Association— Government Practice Section in a half hour continuing legal education program on March 28, 2014. This information theoretically remains available through the Bar Association

8. Son, Daniel Thomas Graham, Iowa law school graduate, 1990

   - Son Dan took the University of Iowa Law School to second place in the National Law School Moot Court contest.

   - Partner in Clark Hill national firm in Chicago. Dan is a recognized very successful trial attorney practicing throughout the entire country.

9. It all started at the University of Iowa Law School.

I will always be proud to be a graduate of the University of Iowa Law School. This is where I obtained the skills, insights, and an opportunity to become the person I was intended to be. As I promised my namesake Msgr. Emmet Kelly, I did my best to make the world I lived in a better place.

Whatever help the Iowa Law School and the Iowa Bar Association can provide to pass on the Land Acquisition Design (LAD) Economic Development–Eminent Domain professional education materials to Iowa's next multiprofessional generation would be appreciated and would continue to help everyone.

There wasn't a single person in the class of 1964 that was not grateful to have had the opportunity to attend the University of Iowa Law School. This is especially true for both James Emmett Graham and his son Daniel Thomas Graham.

...

CPSIA information can be obtained
at www.ICGtesting.com
Printed in the USA
LVOW13*0747280417

532535LV00004B/16/P